GOOD BROTHER, BAD BROTHER

GOOD BROTHER, BAD BROTHER

The Story of Edwin Booth
and John Wilkes Booth

JAMES CROSS GIBLIN

CLARION BOOKS
NEW YORK

Clarion Books
a Houghton Mifflin Company imprint
215 Park Avenue South, New York, NY 10003
Copyright © 2005 by James Cross Giblin

The text was set in 11.5 point Miller Text.
Book design by Carol Goldenberg.

www.houghtonmifflinbooks.com

Printed in the U.S.A.

Library of Congress Cataloging-in-Publication Data

Giblin, James.
Good brother, bad brother : the story of Edwin Booth and John Wilkes Booth /
by James Cross Giblin.
p. cm.
Includes bibliographical references and index.
Audience: Age 10–14.
ISBN 0-618-09642-6
1. Booth, John Wilkes, 1838–1865—Juvenile literature. 2. Booth, John Wilkes, 1838–1865—
Family—Juvenile literature. 3. Booth, Edwin, 1833–1893—Juvenile literature. 4. Assassins—
United States—Biography—Juvenile literature. 5. Actors—United States—Biography—
Juvenile literature. 6. Brothers—United States—Biography—Juvenile literature. 7. Lincoln,
Abraham, 1809–1865—Assassination—Juvenile literature. I. Title.
E457.5.G53 2005
792.02'8'092273—dc22
2004021260

ISBN-13: 978-0-618-09642-8
ISBN-10: 0-618-09642-6

MP 10 9 8 7 6 5 4 3 2 1

To my fellow students in the Drama Department
at Western Reserve University, 1951–54.
We learned so much—and had so much fun!

ACKNOWLEDGMENTS

$\mathcal{G}$RATEFUL THANKS are due the following institutions and individuals for their help in supplying research material and illustrations for the book:

The Library of Congress
The National Archives
The Museum of the City of New York
The Harvard Theatre Collection, Houghton Library
The Library of Performing Arts, New York Public Library
Ford's Theatre, Washington, D.C.
The Players, New York City
The Putnam Publishing Group
Jim Murphy
Terry Alford

The author owes a special debt of gratitude to Michael L. Cooper and Carol Goldenberg, who carried out the illustration research in Washington, D.C., and Cambridge, Massachusetts, respectively.

Contents

GOOD
BROTHER,
BAD BROTHER

Playbill for *The Iron Chest* at the Boston Theatre, April 14, 1865.
The Harvard Theatre Collection, Houghton Library

Chapter 1
A Brother's Crime

Edwin Booth often had premonitions that something bad was going to happen. But there is no evidence that he had any advance warning on April 14, 1865, of the terrible event that was about to befall him and the nation. On that Friday—Good Friday—Booth sat in his dressing room at the Boston Theatre, applying his makeup for the evening performance. The theater's manager had told him the house was sold out, and Booth wanted to give the crowd his best.

An air of eager expectation filled the auditorium as the audience members took their seats in the orchestra or climbed the steep stairs to the balcony. Many had come just to see Booth, who, at thirty-one, was considered one of America's finest actors, if not the finest. But many others had come to celebrate the end of the Civil War.

The Sunday before, on April 9, the Confederate general, Robert E. Lee, had surrendered to the Union commander, Ulysses S. Grant, at the little town of Appomattox Courthouse in Virginia. Four years of increasingly bloody warfare had ended in victory for the North. Now, while the South mourned its loss, people all across the North rejoiced that the fighting was over. The Union flag—the American flag—flew everywhere, and red-white-and-blue bunting decorated lampposts and storefronts in towns large and small.

On Good Friday, thousands of Northerners gave thanks for the victory by attending church services in the morning. Then they flocked to restaurants and saloons to celebrate in other ways. That evening, theaters were packed in cities throughout the North—and Boston was no exception. For the occasion, Edwin Booth, who was famed for his performances in

Shakespeare's plays, chose something in a less classical vein. He decided to appear as the villain, Sir Edward Mortimer, in a melodrama that never failed to please the crowd: *The Iron Chest*.

When Edwin made his entrance, clad in black velvet, the audience greeted him with loud applause. Unlike most actors of his day, Booth never indulged in grand gestures or studied poses. Instead, he acted in a more realistic style, relying on his low, intense voice and piercing dark eyes to compel the spectators' attention. Not a sound could be heard in the vast theater during the climactic death scene, when Booth, as Sir Edward, finally admitted his guilt. And at the end, he was brought back for curtain call after curtain call.

That night Edwin, who was staying at a friend's house in Boston, had trouble getting to sleep. But he still had no intimation of the shock that was in store for him the next morning. Without knocking first, his valet burst into his bedroom shortly after seven. Thrusting a newspaper in front of a dazed Edwin, the man exclaimed, "Mr. Booth, President Lincoln has been shot!" Before Edwin could absorb that terrible fact, the valet went on: "And—oh, Mr. Booth—they say your brother John has done it!"

His brother John . . . how could that be? Edwin knew that John strongly supported the South and hated Abraham Lincoln. He'd often heard John state, without any evidence, that Lincoln would make himself king of the United States if the North won the war. The last time they'd been together, John had stormed out of the room when Edwin, whose sympathies were with the North, told him that he'd voted for Lincoln's reelection. Oh, John could be headstrong. But to shoot the president—to try to kill him? That wasn't the brother he knew and loved.

Edwin grabbed the newspaper from the valet and quickly scanned the story of the shooting, which occupied the entire front page. It said that President Lincoln had been shot and gravely wounded in his box at Ford's Theatre in Washington, where he and his wife had gone to see a play. And there it was, the name of the attacker, who had been recognized at once by many in the audience. He was the dashing, dark-haired young actor who stirred many feminine hearts when he played Romeo in Shakespeare's *Romeo and Juliet* and other romantic roles: John Wilkes Booth.

Later, Edwin would write to a friend that when he saw his brother's name in print, he felt "as if I had been struck on the head by a hammer." As

Edwin Booth.
*Shaw Collection,
The Harvard Theatre
Collection, Houghton Library*

he struggled to comprehend the dreadful news, his mind was a jumble of worries and fears. He thought of his mother, at home in New York with his older sister, Rosalie. John had always been his mother's favorite; how would she deal with the news? Would she have the strength to go on? And where was John now? The newspaper said he had escaped—where had he gone?

While Edwin was still sorting out his reactions and trying to decide what to do, word came that Lincoln had lost his night-long battle for life. The president had died early that morning without ever regaining consciousness. Shortly after that, a messenger arrived with a letter from the manager of the Boston Theatre. "My dear sir," the letter began. "A fearful calamity is upon us. The President of the United States has fallen by the hand of an assassin, and I am shocked to say suspicion points to one nearly related to you as the perpetrator of this horrid deed. God grant it may not prove so!"

But the manager was taking no chances. He went on: "With this knowledge, and out of respect for the anguish which will fill the public mind as soon as the appalling fact shall be fully revealed, I have concluded to close the Boston Theatre until further notice." The manager ended on a cool, impersonal note. "Please signify to me your cooperation in this matter."

Edwin drafted a quick response to the manager's letter. It was written in the formal style of the time, but Edwin's feelings can be sensed between the lines. "With deepest sorrow and great agitation, I thank you for relieving me from my engagement with yourself and the public," he wrote. "The news of the morning has made me wretched indeed, not only because I received the unhappy tidings of the suspicion of a brother's crime, but because a good man, and a most justly honored and patriotic ruler, has fallen by the hand of an assassin."

Edwin concluded the letter with a strong statement of his own loyalty and patriotism. "While mourning, in common with all other loyal hearts, the death of the President, I am oppressed by a private woe not to be expressed in words. But whatever calamity may befall me or mine, my country, one and indivisible, has my warmest devotion."

Now that the Boston Theatre was closed, Edwin had no reason to stay on in Boston. He decided to return to New York as soon as possible and sent a telegram to his mother saying he would take the midnight train and be home on Sunday morning. But he had to delay his departure. Federal marshals wanted to question him about his relations with his brother and what, if anything, he knew about the assassination of the president. They also wanted to conduct a thorough search of his luggage.

Edwin did not keep a diary or journal, so there's no way of knowing what questions the authorities asked him or how he answered them. But an indication of his mood at this time can be glimpsed in a letter he wrote his friend Adam Badeau while waiting for permission to leave Boston.

"My dear Ad," he began. "For the first time since the damnable intelligence stunned me that my brother Wilkes enacted this fearful hellish deed am I able to write. . . . You know, Ad, how I have labored to establish a name that all my friends would be proud of; how I have always toiled for the com-

John Wilkes Booth.
Evert Jansen Wendell Collection, The Harvard Theatre Collection, Houghton Library

Handy

494 Md. Ave, S.W.
WASHINGTON, D.C.

fort and welfare of my family—and how loyal I have been from the first of this damned rebellion [the Civil War]. And you must feel deeply the agony I bear in thus being blasted in all my hopes by a villain [John] who seemed so loveable and in whom all his family found a source of joy in his boyish and confiding nature." Booth ended on a slightly more positive note: "I have a great deal to tell you of myself & the beautiful plans I had for the future— but must wait until my mind is more settled. I am half crazy now—"

The federal marshals found nothing incriminating in Edwin's trunks, or in his correspondence. He was not given clearance to travel, though, until several prominent friends, including the governor of Massachusetts, spoke to the authorities on his behalf. At last, on Easter Sunday afternoon, he received official permission to leave Boston. His friend Orlando Tompkins volunteered to accompany him, and they reserved seats on the midnight train for New York. At that late hour, fewer people would be on the streets and there'd be less chance of Edwin being recognized.

The assassination had aroused strong feelings of outrage throughout the nation. Everyone who had any connection with John came under suspicion, and Edwin's friends feared that the hatred of his brother would rub off on him. Edwin shrugged off their worries. But before leaving for the railroad station, he pulled his wide-brimmed hat down low over his forehead so as to conceal as much of his face as possible.

He and Tompkins boarded the New York train without incident and found their seats in the nearly empty parlor car. Exactly at midnight, the train pulled out of Boston's South Street Station and began the five-and-a-half-hour trip to New York. There's no way of knowing what was on Edwin's mind as he sat back in his seat and stared out into the darkness. No doubt his thoughts centered largely on his brother and the horrible thing he had done. But he must have wondered about his own future, too. Would he ever act again, or would audiences reject him because he was a Booth—the brother of the man who had killed President Lincoln?

A Booth. Earlier he had reminded Adam Badeau how hard he had labored to establish a name that he and all his friends would be proud of. He wasn't the first Booth to do so. Or the first Booth to make his reputation in the theater. His father, the actor Junius Brutus Booth, had emigrated from England in 1821 and, within a short time, had been recognized as one of the finest players American audiences had ever seen.

Edwin always spoke kindly of Junius—his gifted, eccentric, lovable, and often maddening father. Junius had introduced him to the world of the theater and taught him much of what he knew about acting. Now, as he rode southward toward New York and an uncertain future, Edwin may have been wishing his father were still alive to offer advice and support.

Chapter 2
CROWING LIKE A ROOSTER

A METEOR SHOWER BLAZED across the sky above the Maryland farm where Edwin Booth was born on November 13, 1833. And when the baby emerged from the womb, his head was covered with a thin membrane known as a caul. These two things—the meteor shower and the caul—made the superstitious servants think the newborn child would be special. He would have good luck, they said, and would be able to see spirits.

Edwin was named for Edwin Forrest, an American actor whose work his father, Junius, admired. But nothing about the younger Booth suggested that he was destined for a career in the theater. He was a shy, unathletic boy who usually stood to one side when his more active brothers and sisters played games and engaged in horseback-riding contests. He didn't say much during family discussions, either. Instead, he was content to sit back and listen, observing the others with his large, dark eyes.

Edwin was the seventh of ten children in the Booth family, six of whom lived to adulthood. The other four all died before the age of twelve, victims of diseases like measles and smallpox that carried off so many children in the nineteenth century. Edwin had an older brother, the sturdy, muscular Junius, who was named for his father, and an older sister, Rosalie. After Edwin came another sister, Asia, named for the continent where her father thought the Garden of Eden had been located. "It's where Man first walked with God," the elder Booth often said.

Following Asia came two more brothers—John Wilkes, who was his parents' favorite from the day he was born, and Joseph. John had a famous namesake, the eighteenth-century British radical John Wilkes, who opposed the king and fought for the rights of the common people. John Wilkes was also a distant relative of Junius Brutus Booth's. There was a wide age range among the six surviving Booth children: Junius Jr. was twelve years older than Edwin, and John Wilkes and Joseph were five and seven years younger.

In the winter months, when their actor father was off performing in theaters across the country, the Booth children with their mother moved into a house in Baltimore. There they attended school and enjoyed the benefits of city life. But they all looked forward to summer, when the theaters closed—there was no way to cool them in the days before air-conditioning—and Mr. Booth came home. Then they would pack up their clothes and other belongings and move back to the estate, consisting of 150 acres of woods and farmland, that Mr. Booth had purchased in the Maryland countryside near the village of Bel Air. He added onto the log house that

Tudor Hall, the home of the Booth family. *The Museum of the City of New York*

came with the property and made it into a comfortable home that he named Tudor Hall.

Junius Booth Sr. was happiest when he was at Tudor Hall. In fact, some thought his favorite role was not a king in one of Shakespeare's plays but a farmer raising a bountiful crop of vegetables and fruits. He did not leave their cultivation to his hired hands but worked in the fields himself, hoeing the soil and pulling up weeds. As soon as they were old enough, all his children were expected to join in the work. And when it was time to harvest the crops, the Booth children helped their father load what the family didn't need into a wagon and sell it at the open-air farmers' market in Baltimore.

Mr. Booth believed that all life must be sacred since it came from the Almighty. He forbade the killing of any living creature on the farm, and would not allow the branding of cattle for fear that it might hurt them. In line with these beliefs, he was a strict vegetarian and insisted that his children, too, refrain from eating meat. He also refused to own slaves even though the practice was common in Maryland, a border state between North and South, in the years before the Civil War. Instead, Mr. Booth hired free blacks to help with the work on the farm.

Life at Tudor Hall was not all chores, though. Mr. Booth enjoyed playing with his children and encouraging their interests in nature and literature. In the evening, Edwin and his brothers and sisters often gathered around their father and mother in the front parlor. Although he had never gone to college, Mr. Booth owned an extensive library. By the light of an oil lamp, he would read aloud from one of his books—a play by Shakespeare, or the poetry of Keats and Shelley, or a classic work by Milton, Dante, or Plutarch. Edwin thrilled when his father used his magnificent voice to conjure up Dante's terrifying vision of Hell.

Besides introducing his children to great works of literature, Mr. Booth told them stories from his own colorful youth in England. He had dropped out of school at an early age, disappointing his lawyer father. After brief apprenticeships with a printer, an architect, and a sculptor, the young Booth left home and joined a troupe of traveling actors. The troupe played the English provinces, performing in tents pitched in village squares on market days and on platforms set up in the fields at county fairs. Wherever they went, Booth and his fellow players had to compete with other travel-

Junius Brutus Booth
as a young man.
Painting by John Vanderlyn.
The Library of Congress

ing performers: jugglers, trained dogs, strongmen displaying their muscles, and walkers on stilts.

After their season in the provinces ended, Junius and the others in the troupe crossed the English Channel and embarked on a tour of Holland and Belgium. By the time he returned to England, Booth had graduated from small parts to larger ones, and then to leading roles. He was short, only a little more than five feet, and noticeably bowlegged—one night a spectator in the first row called out, "Ah, you'd be a pretty fellow to stop a pig!" But his handsome face, commanding gaze, and powerful voice made audiences forget his curved legs and small stature. As his fellow actor Joseph Jefferson said, Booth "had the look of an uncaged tiger and seemed to snap with fire" when he was onstage.

Junius Brutus Booth as Posthumus in *Cymbeline* by William Shakespeare.
The Library of Congress

Edwin, Asia, John, and the other Booth children loved to hear their father talk about his early stage triumphs. They also enjoyed the story of how he had met their mother. One day in London, Booth had noticed a black-haired young woman selling flowers from a stall near the Covent Garden Theatre, where he was performing. He introduced himself and she recognized his name. In fact, she had seen him play King Lear just the week before. But she could hardly believe that the handsome young man standing before her and the battered old king she'd seen onstage were one and the same.

After a brief conversation—during which Junius learned that her name was Mary Ann Holmes—he asked, "When will you have a day to spend with me? Tomorrow perhaps?" Before she knew what she was saying, Mary Ann replied, "Yes—tomorrow." That was the beginning of a relationship that before long led to marriage, and then to the decision to seek their fortune in America. They settled in Maryland, and soon afterward the first of their children was born. It made a lovely, romantic story, and one that Edwin and the others enjoyed hearing over and over again. Only later did they discover that it wasn't exactly the whole truth about their parents' past lives—especially their father's.

There were other things they didn't know about their father until disturbing reports reached them of his strange behavior on the road. When Junius was away from his family, and moving quickly by train and coach from one city to another, he often got lonely. The feeling was particularly acute after a performance. He would be on a high, having given his all to the audience, but there was no one he felt close to with whom he could relax until he was ready for bed and sleep. At those times, Junius turned more and more frequently to a bottle of whiskey for companionship. Sometimes he would wander far from his hotel in the quest for another drink, and would fail to turn up the next day for a rehearsal or performance.

But that wasn't the worst of it. If he had drunk too much, he would sometimes do crazy things. In Boston, in the middle of a performance of Shakespeare's *Hamlet,* Booth suddenly turned to the audience and shouted, "I can't read! I'm a charity boy! I can't read! Take me to the lunatic asylum!"

The theater manager hurried him offstage, still shouting, and another actor replaced him. But Booth's spell of insanity wasn't over yet. He ripped off his costume in the dressing room, sneaked out of the theater, and set off on foot for Providence, Rhode Island, fifty miles away and the next stop on his tour. The driver of the Boston-to-Providence coach saw him striding along the side of the road in his stocking feet, wearing only his underwear and reciting poetry in a loud voice.

Another time, when he was performing Hamlet in Natchez, Mississippi, Booth could not be found at the start of Act V. The other actors began the act without him but were interrupted by the sound of a rooster crowing high above the stage. When they looked up, they saw Booth perched atop a ladder, smiling broadly as he crowed merrily on. The performance came to a halt while the stage manager climbed the ladder. After a lengthy discussion, Booth agreed to come down and continue the play—but only after the stage manager promised that he could climb the ladder and start crowing again as soon as the play was over.

Word of such incidents spread, and Booth soon gained a reputation for being unreliable. Managers continued to hire him, however, because he always drew a crowd. Still they knew, as did his family, that his unpredictable behavior could not be tolerated indefinitely. Eventually he would have to change his ways, or run the risk of permanent banishment from the theater.

Today an actor with a problem like Junius Booth's would probably seek help from a psychiatrist or some other mental health professional. But there were no such specialists in Booth's time. Instead, it was up to Mary Ann and his children to find a way to deal with what they called "Father's calamity." Mary Ann decided the best course of action would be for the oldest boy, Junius Jr.—whom everyone in the family called June—to go on the road with his father. June could take care of his costumes and props, help him with his travel arrangements, and be company for him after his performances and on the long trips between cities. He could also do his best to keep his father from drinking too much. And he would be on hand to bring him back to sanity if he veered off into one of his crazy spells.

June did a fine job helping his father stay on track, but he was only willing to do it for so long. He was in his twenties now, and had begun to build a theatrical career of his own, first as an actor and then as a theater manager. He had also met a young woman he wanted to marry. But Mary Ann was fearful of letting Junius travel by himself again. Despite June's careful attention, his father still managed to slip away occasionally and go on a binge. He also had more than a few bouts of madness, especially after an unexpected visitor arrived from England in 1846.

The visitor was Adelaide Booth, Junius's first wife. Her existence was unknown to everyone at Tudor Hall except Mary Ann, who had been so in love with Junius that she had accompanied him to America even though she'd known he was already married.

Adelaide, in turn, knew nothing of Junius's American family, which he had kept secret from her for twenty-five years. It might have remained a secret if Junius and Adelaide's son, Richard, hadn't discovered his father's other family during a visit to America the year before. He had written his mother to tell her of his discovery, and Adelaide had made arrangements to sail to America as soon as she could. Now she was in Baltimore, ready to confront the husband who had abandoned her a quarter of a century earlier. In a stormy meeting, she demanded that Junius acknowledge her as his one true wife, and Richard as his only legitimate son.

Booth was in no mood to disown his beloved Mary Ann along with Edwin, Asia, June, and his other American children. He angrily reminded Adelaide that he had supported her and Richard with regular and generous payments over the years, and had provided additional funds for Richard's education. When she repeated her demand that he publicly recognize her as his only legal wife, he told her he wanted nothing more to do with her. She could either return at once to England or sue him for divorce.

Adelaide chose to remain in Baltimore and file for divorce, charging adultery. While her suit was pending, she did her best to make life miserable for Junius and Mary Ann, denouncing them whenever she got the chance. Mary Ann tried to shield the younger children from what was going on, but the older children, including Edwin and Asia, couldn't help but be affected by their father's marital problems. None of them ever commented directly on their own feelings during this painful period. But Asia, in a biography she wrote of her father after his death, passed off his marriage to Adelaide as a boyish mistake. Edwin, in an interview years later, simply denied that Junius had ever been married to anyone except Edwin's mother, Mary Ann.

Adelaide's divorce from Junius Brutus Booth was granted at last in April 1851, and he and Mary Ann Holmes were married again in Baltimore on

May 10—which happened to be their son John Wilkes's thirteenth birthday. Edwin was seventeen by then, and already well on his way toward a career in the theater. After his brother June had stopped serving as companion and watchdog to his father four years earlier, there had seemed to be only one person who could replace June—his younger brother Edwin. And so, at age thirteen, Edwin had put his childhood behind him and set out on the first of many theatrical tours he would make with his father.

Chapter 3
"WHERE ARE YOUR SPURS?"

𝓔DWIN HADN'T WANTED to go on the road with the great Junius Brutus Booth. Much as he loved his father, he would have preferred staying on at school in Baltimore, and continuing to take violin lessons with his music teacher, Signor Picioli. Earlier, one of the field hands at Tudor Hall had taught Edwin to play the banjo, and he enjoyed making music for his family and friends.

Junius had never encouraged Edwin to pursue a career in the theater, either. Quite the contrary; he had suggested more than once that Edwin should learn to work with his hands and become a master carpenter and cabinetmaker. It was a much steadier profession, he said. But Junius needed a companion on the road to help him stay out of trouble, and young Edwin was the only likely candidate.

His mother urged Edwin to accept the assignment, saying he could take his schoolbooks along and study them in his spare moments. That was easier said than done, however, for Edwin had virtually no free time. From early morning until late at night, he was busy with one task after another. If it was a traveling day, he helped his father pack his clothes, costumes, and props. Then he shouldered his share of the luggage as they journeyed from one city to another by train, boat, or horse-drawn carriage.

If it was a performance day, he sat off to one side while Junius rehearsed that night's play with the other actors. A mid-nineteenth-century star like Junius knew by heart the leading roles in many plays by Shakespeare and other well-known dramatists. During a four- or five-night stay in a city such as Pittsburgh or Cleveland, he might play the villainous Richard III in Shakespeare's drama of the same name on the first night, Hamlet on the second, King Lear on the third, and then repeat Richard III—the role for which he was best known—on the fourth night.

Junius, like other stars of the time, usually traveled without a troupe of other performers. Local actors from each community where he played would be engaged to support him. Like the star, the local performers were expected to know their lines in a number of different plays and be able to shift roles on a day's notice or less. They, and the star, would be lucky if they managed to get through one complete rehearsal of the play before they went on for that evening's performance.

This method of working was cheaper than sending a complete troupe of well-rehearsed actors on tour, but it often resulted in a sloppy performance. Neither audiences nor actors seemed to mind. Both took it for granted that this was the way things were done in the theater. Some beginners were confused, however. One young actor apologized profusely to Junius after a rehearsal in which he entered from the wrong side of the stage. "It makes no difference to me, young man," Junius said with a smile. "Just come out. I'll find you!"

The fast pace of touring meant Junius had to rehearse by himself, with Edwin's assistance. At breakfast, over lunch, and during long train rides, Junius would often ask Edwin to read the other characters' lines to him so that he could refresh his memory of his own part. In the course of these sessions, Edwin came to know his father's roles almost as well as Junius did.

Edwin's busiest time occurred before each performance. It was his job to lay out his father's costumes for the evening's play and help him into them. If Junius wore a wig for the part, Edwin brushed it and put it carefully in place. On the nights that Junius played the hunchbacked Richard III, Edwin made sure that the padded lump on Junius's back was firmly fastened. He would never forget the night the padding had fallen off during a fight scene and the audience had roared with laughter. Only after Junius kicked the padding offstage and shouted his next line was quiet restored. But Junius himself was anything but quiet when he thundered offstage at intermission, demanding to know why Edwin hadn't tied the padding more tightly.

Edwin's workday usually ended when the final curtain came down and Junius took his last bow. But some nights it was just beginning. Edwin recognized the warning signs: His father would sit heavily at the makeup table

Junius Brutus Booth in costume for one of his roles.
The Library of Congress

in his dressing room, yank off his helmet or wig, and try to dismiss Edwin with a wave of his hand. "Go away, young man, go away!" he would say in a commanding voice. Edwin always stood his ground, knowing his father would head off to the nearest saloon if no one was there to stop him.

Junius didn't cease trying to get around Edwin, though. One night in Louisville, Kentucky, after giving a particularly intense performance as Richard III, Junius ripped off his costume and strode out the dressing room door. He called back over his shoulder that he was going for a walk. Edwin bolted after him, saying he wanted to walk too. With Junius leading the way, they commenced a kind of race through the midnight streets of the city.

Sometimes Junius would run on ahead, wait until Edwin had almost caught up with him, then dart down a deserted side street. When he came to an open-air market covered by a tin roof, Junius paced its entire length at a rapid clip, with Edwin close on his heels. Then he swung around, glared at his son, and strode back the way he had come, moving at an even faster pace. Edwin was not about to concede defeat. He matched his father step for step, and the two of them marched back and forth, back and forth between the empty market stalls.

They didn't stop until the first rays of dawn brightened the eastern sky. At that point an exhausted Junius suddenly called a halt to their test of wills, and an equally exhausted Edwin followed suit a moment later. Neither of them said anything as they leaned against adjoining stalls, catching their breaths. Then Edwin led the way back to their hotel, where they fell silently onto their beds without bothering to get out of their clothes.

Fortunately, there weren't many sleepless nights like that one. As the years passed, Junius strayed less frequently and the bond between father and son grew stronger. By now it was 1849, and Edwin was fifteen. He didn't have a very high opinion of his adolescent appearance. "I was a sight," he said later to his friend the drama critic William Winter. "I wore my hair down to my shoulders like a woman. I had a sallow complexion and a thin face and went around looking like a crushed tragedian."

Others had a very different impression of the young Edwin. In his autobiography, Joseph Jefferson said Edwin was "the handsomest boy I remember ever to have seen. With his dark hair and deep eyes he was like one of [the artist Bartolomé] Murillo's Italian peasant boys."

After all the hours he had spent sitting in on rehearsals and watching performances from the wings, it was almost inevitable that Edwin would one day go on the stage himself. That day came on September 10, 1849, a little more than two months before his sixteenth birthday. Edwin and his father were in Boston, where Junius was scheduled to play Richard III at the Boston Museum. (The Boston Museum was so named because some city residents, influenced by Puritan ideas, were reluctant to enter a building called a theater.) The overworked stage manager at the theater complained that he had been assigned to play too many small parts in the production in addition to his regular backstage duties. He suggested that Edwin

The teenaged Edwin Booth on tour with his father.
Evert Jansen Wendell Collection, The Harvard Theatre Collection,
Houghton Library

replace him in the role of Tressel, and Junius agreed to the substitution.

The theater manager, sensing a chance to get some additional publicity, made a point of announcing the cast change on the playbill:

DUKE OF GLOSTER, AFTERWARDS KING RICHARD III .... MR. BOOTH
TRESSEL, *(his 1st appearance on any stage)* .... EDWIN BOOTH

Edwin never commented on his feelings that day. But much later he did tell William Winter how his father had helped him prepare for his debut. The two of them were in Junius's dressing room before the performance, Junius sitting at his makeup table and Edwin standing to one side, dressed in Tressel's black costume.

"Who was Tressel?" Junius asked.

"A messenger from the battlefield of Tewksbury."

"What was his mission?" Junius continued.

"To bear the news of the defeat of the king's party."

"How did he make the journey?"

"On horseback," Edwin replied promptly.

Junius fixed his son with a hard gaze and asked, "Then where are your spurs?"

Edwin's voice quavered. "I hadn't thought of them."

"Forgot them, did you?" Junius said with a slight smile. "Here, take mine."

Edwin unbuckled his father's spurs and fastened them onto his own boots. Then he hurried downstairs to the stage so he would be ready when the cue came for his entrance.

Not everyone was impressed by Edwin's first stage appearance. Rufus Choate, a former senator, was sitting in one of the front rows. After Edwin had delivered his message and left the stage, Choate was heard to whisper to his companion, "It's a great pity that eminent men should have such mediocre children."

But Edwin himself felt more confident. When he rejoined his father in his dressing room and Junius asked, "Have you done well?" Edwin replied, "I think so."

"Then give me back my spurs," Junius said.

From that modest start, Edwin soon graduated to larger roles. On September 27, in Providence, Rhode Island, he played a major part in support of his father in Shakespeare's *Othello*. Within a few months he added roles in Shakespeare's *King Lear* and *The Merchant of Venice* to his fast-growing repertory. He also took on parts in a number of lesser-known plays.

Junius put up no objections to Edwin's developing career as an actor, and he stopped talking about cabinetmaking as a possible occupation for his son. But he offered Edwin no special assistance, either. "He never gave me instruction, professional advice, or encouragement in any form," Edwin wrote later in a letter to William Winter. "He had, doubtless, resolved to make me work my way unaided; and although his seeming indifference was painful then, it compelled me to exercise my callow wits. It made me think."

One day Junius and Edwin, performing together in New York City, ran into an old acquaintance of Junius's on Broadway. "Upon which of your sons do you intend to confer your mantle?" the friend asked.

Junius said nothing, but he laid a hand on top of Edwin's head.

"He had to reach up," Edwin remembered later. At sixteen, he was already taller than his father.

During the next few years, Edwin continued to tour with Junius and to play an ever-greater assortment of roles. Then came the night when, with virtually no rehearsal, he took the giant step of going on for his father as Richard III. It was April 1851, and the Booths were performing in New York. One afternoon Junius woke from a nap in his hotel room and declared that he "didn't feel like acting" that night.

"What will they do without you?" Edwin asked.

"Go act it yourself."

Edwin left reluctantly for the theater. He dreaded telling the manager that Junius would not perform that night and was sure the manager would never accept Junius's suggestion that he, Edwin, replace his father. But the manager surprised him. "No matter," the man said coolly. "You play Richard. Or else we'll have to close the house."

Without giving himself time to think, Edwin got into his father's costume, which was several sizes too big for him because Junius was heavier. In the half hour before curtain time, Edwin read quickly through the script, remembering how his father acted certain key moments. Then he was led down to the stage, where one of the other actors listened as he hastily recited Richard's first long speech. Fortunately, the words came back to him from all the nights he had watched his father deliver them.

Now there was no time left. As the curtain rose, Edwin checked to make sure the padding on his back was firmly in place. Then he bent over in the position Junius always assumed when he played Richard and hobbled out onto the stage. There had been no announcement that he was replacing his father, and a rustling sound came from the auditorium as the people in the audience checked their playbills. The noise stopped, however, when Edwin spoke his first lines, forcing his light voice down a notch or two to approximate his father's deeper register.

He got through Richard's first soliloquy, and the next scene, and the scene after that. Only a few times did the prompter have to feed him his lines. As his confidence grew, he began to feel his command over the audience. When, alone onstage, he twisted his face into a sneer as he announced the next step in Richard's evil scheme to gain power, he could sense the audience shudder in horror.

After the final curtain fell and the auditorium erupted in applause, the theater manager hurried onstage. He grabbed Edwin by the arm and led him out in front of the curtain. As Edwin bowed, and bowed again, the applause rose to an even greater pitch. The manager beamed. "You see before you the worthy scion of a noble stock," he said, referring to Edwin's father, and many in the audience shouted their assent.

Edwin could still hear the audience's applause when he returned to the hotel where he and his father were staying. "Well, how did it go?" his father asked when Edwin came through the door. Junius lay stretched out on his bed exactly as Edwin had left him. But something about the expression on his face made Edwin think his father had gone to the theater and seen the performance, and managed to get back to the hotel just before Edwin arrived. He could never be certain, though.

That spring Edwin signed a contract on his own with a Baltimore theater to play a variety of roles for six dollars a week. But the following season he went out on the road again with his father. Then in May 1852, his older brother June came home to Maryland for a visit. June had an unusual proposition to make to his father—one that would change Junius's life, and Edwin's also.

June had found his way to San Francisco, booming in the wake of the gold rush of 1849. There he had been hired to manage the city's newest theater, the Jenny Lind, named for the Swedish singer who had just toured the United States to great acclaim. Now June had made the long trip back east to persuade Junius to come to San Francisco. People there and in the gold-fields were starved for entertainment, June told his father. He could make a fortune if he returned with June to the West.

The money was appealing, but it was the longing for new experiences that led Junius to accept his son's invitation. Junius was growing older—he was fifty-six now—and he thought this trip to the West might be his last chance for adventure. He made preparations to leave with June for San Francisco at the end of May. Mary Ann would stay behind to run the farm with the help of Edwin and her other children.

When Junius and June got to New York City on the first leg of their trip, Junius ran into some old theater friends and disappeared. By the time he was located in a bar on the Bowery, he and June had missed the boat. Realizing that he needed Edwin to keep him in line, Junius went back to Maryland and persuaded his younger son to accompany him to San Francisco. Junius still required a chaperon, and no one could fill that role better than Edwin.

Chapter 4
GOLD PIECES AND BLIZZARDS

───────────────────────────

❧❧❧

THERE WAS NO QUICK or easy way to get from the East Coast to California in 1852. Air travel existed only in fantasy, and the first transcontinental railroad would not be completed until 1869. Travelers to the West had their choice of three possible routes: a hard and dangerous trek by land across barren deserts and towering mountain ranges; a long sea voyage around South America; or a shorter voyage via the Isthmus of Panama.

The Booths chose the third route. They took a steamship from New York to Panama, where they left the ship and crossed the isthmus by canoe and on muleback—the Panama Canal was still just a dream. When they reached the Pacific Ocean, they boarded another steamship for the trip up along the coast of Mexico to California. The Booths left New York in early June and didn't arrive in San Francisco until July 28.

Edwin had never seen anything like the booming city by the bay. Lavishly furnished hotels and restaurants stood next to flimsy wooden and canvas shacks where trinkets from the Far East were sold. Grizzled miners sporting gold chains and diamond rings lounged on the wooden sidewalks outside the doors of crowded saloons. Elaborately decorated horse-drawn carriages raced along the streets, throwing up clouds of dust on dry days and splattering mud when it rained.

June led his father and brother to his home atop Telegraph Hill and made preparations for their debut at the Jenny Lind Theater in the popular melodrama *The Iron Chest*. Junius and Edwin played a two-week season to sold-out crowds, ending with Junius giving his all in the title role of Shakespeare's *Macbeth*. June could easily have extended their stay in San Francisco, but the Jenny Lind was about to be turned into the city hall, and

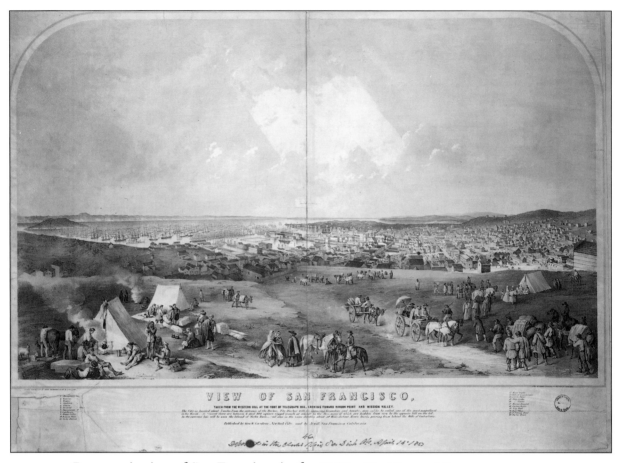

Panoramic view of San Francisco in the 1850s. *The Library of Congress*

no other theater was available. So he made arrangements for them to travel on to Sacramento, ten hours upriver by steamboat.

Sacramento was smaller and rougher than San Francisco, and closer to the goldfields. When the miners went to the theater in San Francisco, they wore their best suits; in Sacramento, they came straight from the mines in their dirty work clothes. San Francisco was famed for the rats that roamed its streets. Sacramento was notorious for the bedbugs that infested its boarding houses and hotels.

Once again the Booths began their run with *The Iron Chest,* and it went over as well with the opening night crowd in Sacramento as it had in San Francisco. But the size of their audiences dropped off noticeably after that.

This was not due to any fault of theirs—Junius and Edwin were acting as well as ever—but to one of the sudden depressions that hit the gold country every now and then. A wave of pessimism swept over the miners, and those who had money cut back on their spending.

Faced with declining box-office receipts, the Booths put on benefit performances for themselves. At such performances, which were common in the nineteenth-century theater, one of the actors took home the bulk of the evening's receipts. Some benefit performances were given to honor an aging actor, or to aid a player who had fallen on hard times. In the case of the Booths, the benefits helped them make up for their losses in earnings due to thin crowds.

For his benefit, Edwin chose to play the villainous Jaffier in Thomas Otway's seventeenth-century tragedy, *Venice Preserved*. When his father saw Edwin in Jaffier's costume of black tunic and tights, he said, "You look like Hamlet. Why didn't you play him tonight?"

"If I ever have another benefit I will," Edwin replied.

Following their last performance in Sacramento, the Booths packed their bags and returned to San Francisco. There Junius told June that he had had enough of California. Instead of the fortune he'd expected to make, he had almost nothing to show for his efforts. He agreed to a farewell engagement of four performances in San Francisco, but then, he said, he wanted to go home by the next ship.

Edwin offered to return to Maryland with his father, but Junius advised him to stay on in California and perfect his craft. He'd never be able to develop his own acting style, Junius said, until he struck out on his own and stopped imitating his father. Before leaving, Junius asked Dave Anderson, an old friend and fellow actor, to keep an eye on Edwin and help him along. That done, Junius set sail on the *Independence*, bound for Nicaragua in Central America. He waved a cheery goodbye to Edwin and June as the ship pulled away from the dock.

After Junius's departure, Edwin, now nineteen, drifted around San Francisco for a while. The economic depression had spread to the city, and jobs were hard to come by. Then he received an offer to join a troupe that was about to leave on a tour of the northern California mining camps. Eager for work, Edwin signed on at once. His brother June, knowing the hardships such a tour might involve, drew him aside and said, "Put a slug

Junius Brutus Booth at the time of the California trip. *The Library of Congress*

[a piece of gold worth fifty dollars] in the bottom of your trunk, forget you have it, and when things are at their worst bring out your slug." Edwin took June's advice and hid a slug in his suitcase before leaving San Francisco.

The troupe steamed upriver to Sacramento, and then up the Feather River to the town of Marysville. There they climbed into stagecoaches for the journey into the mountains on narrow, winding roads. Now and then a grizzly bear crossed their path. The troupe's first stop was Nevada City, a cluster of wooden shacks set amid towering pines. From there they went on to Grass Valley and Rough and Ready and Downieville, located at the bottom of a mountain valley.

Sometimes they played in a real theater with a sign out front proclaiming it was the "Nevada City Opera House" or the "Downieville Dramatic Hall." More often they acted on a wooden platform set up at the end of a saloon, warehouse, or barn. Wherever they went, they found an enthusiastic audience of miners. In the mid-nineteenth century, long before radio, the movies, and television were invented, live theater was one of the few forms of popular entertainment. That explains why even remote mining towns like Rough and Ready had makeshift theaters.

Crude the theaters might be, but the audiences that filled them were not ignorant. Their faces might be weathered, their clothes shabby, but many of them had read the plays of Shakespeare and other classic writers. If Edwin and his fellow actors flubbed a line or skipped an important passage, the audience was quick to jeer and stamp its feet. But if they played well and spoke all the lines clearly and with feeling, the audience showed its appreciation by tossing gold pieces at them.

The troupe was finishing a successful stay in Downieville when an early blizzard buried the town in snow. The actors managed to make their way back to Grass Valley, where food was in short supply and incredibly expensive. To feed the entire troupe, Edwin dug down in his suitcase and fished out the slug he'd brought along for just such an emergency.

Their spirits restored by a good meal, the actors started out for Nevada City. They hoped to put on some shows there and make enough money to pay for the steamer trip home. But when they finally got to Nevada City, they found all the town's businesses, including the theater, closed by the storm. None of the miners in the surrounding goldfields could get to town to spend their money.

The troupe checked into Nevada City's only hotel while they decided what to do next. That evening Edwin went for a walk by himself along the deserted main street. When he started back, he saw one of his fellow actors, George Spear, running toward him through the darkness. "Ted, is that you?" he called. Ted was Edwin's nickname.

"Yes, what's up?"

"There's a mail just in, and a message for you," Spear replied.

"What does it say?"

"Not good news, my boy."

Edwin, who often had premonitions, sensed what the message said. "Spear," he asked, "is my father dead?"

Spear simply nodded.

Edwin began to sob. "I should have gone with him, I should have gone with him!" he wailed over and over as George Spear led him back to the hotel. There he learned that his brother June had sent the manager of the troupe the message about their father's death. June had asked that one of the actors inform Edwin, thinking it might be easier if he heard the dreadful news from a friend instead of simply reading it.

At this dark moment, Edwin had an intense longing to be with his brother, his only relative on the West Coast. He also wanted to find out more about Junius's death: Where had he died, and how? And could he, Edwin, have done anything to prevent it if he'd been with him? When he heard the next morning that a party was going to try to plow through the snowdrifts and reach Marysville, fifty miles down the road, he immediately made plans to join the group.

The travelers would be on foot, so Edwin arranged for his trunk to be shipped to San Francisco later and carried with him only what was absolutely necessary. The men in the party trudged single file through the snow, each one putting his feet in the prints of the man in front. They stayed overnight in a miner's shack and pushed on to Marysville the next day, arriving just before nightfall. Edwin borrowed ten dollars from one of the other travelers and bought a steamboat ticket to Sacramento, and from there to San Francisco.

When he got to June's house, the two brothers hugged each other and shared their memories of the last time they had seen their father. Then Edwin sat down to read two letters that had come from their mother. In them she told her sons everything she knew about the sad circumstances that had led to Junius's death. The facts were painful to read, but Edwin didn't rise from his chair until he had digested them all.

After leaving San Francisco, his father had made it safely to a port on the Pacific coast of Nicaragua. He crossed that tropical country by stagecoach and boarded another ship that took him across the Gulf of Mexico to New Orleans. Somewhere along the way, though, most of his California earnings were stolen. A sympathetic theater manager in New Orleans arranged for him to play a series of six performances there so he could recoup the money he had lost. With more than a thousand dollars to show for his efforts, Junius then booked passage on a steamboat bound for Cincinnati up the Mississippi River.

Unfortunately, he had caught a severe cold in New Orleans. It made him so thirsty that he ignored warnings and drank several glasses of polluted river water. By evening he had developed a high fever. It worsened the next day, weakening him to such an extent that he was unable to leave his cabin. A fellow passenger, James Simpson, had recognized Booth in the dining salon on the first day out, and noticed his absence on the second day. He went by Booth's cabin to check on him and found the actor in a near-delirious state.

There was no doctor on the boat, but Simpson ministered to Booth as best he could. He summoned a porter to clean the actor's cabin and change his soiled bed linen. By the third day, Booth's jaws had begun to stiffen. Unable to find any medical supplies, Simpson soaked a clean cloth in brandy and tried to force it between the actor's clenched teeth. Booth pushed the cloth away, saying, "No more in this world."

Simpson feared the situation was hopeless and asked Booth if he wanted to send a message to his wife. In a weak voice, the actor whispered, "Oh, that I could talk!" On the fifth day, Simpson spent all morning with Booth until the dinner bell rang at noon. Simpson got up to leave, and Booth called after him, "Pray—pray—pray!" Those were the last words Junius Brutus Booth ever spoke. The renowned actor died at one o'clock that afternoon as the boat was approaching Louisville, Kentucky.

All of this Edwin's mother recounted in the first of the letters to her sons. She had received word of her husband's death by telegram, and had journeyed to Cincinnati to claim his body. While there, she had also had a chance to talk with his last companion, the kindly Simpson. Then she had returned to Baltimore by train, taking Junius's body home for burial.

After finishing the letter, Edwin's first impulse was to return to Maryland and help his mother manage the family farm. But he changed his mind once he had read her second letter. He wasn't needed in Maryland, she said. She planned to rent out the Baltimore house and make their country place into a year-round home. Johnnie, as she and the others in the family called the young John Wilkes, was fourteen now, old enough to help with the farm chores. And Asia, Rosalie, and Joseph could make themselves useful, too.

What Mrs. Booth didn't say was that she had virtually no cash on hand. The thousand dollars Junius had earned in New Orleans was not in his wallet when he died. Obviously, someone besides Simpson had gotten into his cabin and picked his pocket while he was sleeping. Mrs. Booth deliberately refrained from telling Edwin and June of her financial problems, however. She wanted both of her older sons to have the chance to stay on in California and seek their fortunes.

Edwin and June were more than ready to comply with their mother's wishes—especially Edwin. Having tasted one brief period of freedom in the mountains, he was eager to see where his talent and questing spirit would take him next.

Chapter 5
HAMLET IN HONOLULU

$\mathcal{S}$INCE COMING TO SAN FRANCISCO, Edwin had been staying with June. But now, in the wake of his father's death, he wanted to be on his own. He joined forces with his father's old friend Dave Anderson, and together they moved into a house—a two-room shack, really—out in the sand dunes beyond Mission Dolores. In the city directory, they called the house a "ranch" and listed themselves as "comedians and rancheros."

Edwin also adopted the clothing of a ranchero. When he rode into town on a white horse, borrowed from June, he made a dashing impression in a black slouch hat, high black boots, and a Spanish-style cloak worn over a bright-red shirt. Young women, and older ones as well, responded to his appearance and wanted to get to know him better. Theater audiences responded to him too, and applauded him in a variety of plays ranging from rowdy farces to Shakespeare's tragedies.

Edwin was a member of the acting company at the San Francisco Theater, which had just been remodeled and freshly painted. But so many miners in the audience chewed and spat tobacco that the floors and lower walls of the auditorium were soon stained brown. The smell got so bad that patrons complained, and June had to close the theater for a thorough cleaning and airing. When it reopened, the first attraction was a new production of Shakespeare's *Hamlet*.

Edwin lobbied for a chance to perform the title role. June hesitated at first; he still wasn't convinced that his younger brother took acting seriously. But Edwin persisted, telling June that no less an authority than their father had said he should play the part. In the end, June gave in, and

Painting of the young Edwin Booth in the role of Hamlet. *The Library of Congress*

posters went up throughout the city announcing that on April 25, 1853, Mr. Edwin Booth would play Hamlet for the first time.

The response of the city's theater critics was encouraging. In the *Daily Alta California*, Ferdinand C. Ewer wrote: "The favorite play of *Hamlet* was produced at the San Francisco Theater last night, Mr. Booth supporting the principal part and making his first appearance in that difficult character.

As a first appearance, it may be considered highly creditable, and we can even predict a high degree of success for the promising young artist when he shall have overcome a few disagreeable faults in intonation and delivery, and reached a profound conception of the part."

After Hamlet, Edwin took on leading roles in other classic plays of Shakespeare: Benedick in *Much Ado About Nothing*, Romeo in *Romeo and Juliet*, and even Shylock, the middle-aged main character in *The Merchant of Venice*. He also appeared in a number of popular comedies and melodramas—such as *The Honeymoon, The Belle's Stratagem, Who's Got the Countess?*—none of which are remembered today. And all of this when he was not yet twenty!

Following in his late father's footsteps, Edwin also started to drink more than he should. Perhaps this was due to youthful cockiness. Or perhaps alcohol helped to ease the pressures of his heavy work schedule, which involved learning the lines of one leading character after another. In a letter written years later to William Winter, Edwin offered a harsh description of himself at this time: "At twenty, I was a libertine," he wrote. "I knew no better. Sin was in me and it consumed me while it was shut up close, so I let it out and it seemed to rage and burn. All the vices seemed to have full sway over me."

Whatever the cause, Edwin's drinking began to affect his performances. Ferdinand Ewer, who had praised the young actor's Hamlet, now advised him to study his parts more carefully. Another critic was less gentle. Reviewing Edwin's performance in a play called *The Queen's Husband*, this critic wrote that "Mr. Booth was . . . habitually spirited." That was another way of saying he was obviously drunk.

Most of the time Edwin's drinking was not that noticeable, however. He retained his popularity with San Francisco theatergoers and continued to get steady work. In the spring of 1854 he was hired to act opposite the well-known English actress Laura Keene when she made her San Francisco debut in a romantic comedy, *The Love Chase*.

Talented and hot tempered, Laura Keene was one of the most intriguing personalities in the mid-nineteenth-century theater. Her early life gave little indication that she was destined for a career on the stage. Born to a poor London family in 1826, Keene began her working life as a barmaid in one of the city's many taverns. She quickly won the affection of the bar's patrons, who called her "Red Laura" because of her auburn-colored hair. They also enjoyed her recitations. An avid reader, Keene liked to declaim passages from Shakespeare's plays and sonnets while she served drinks.

Keene was married at an early age to a British army officer, John Taylor, who opened his own tavern after he was discharged from the service. Laura helped him in the business when she wasn't busy taking care of their two young daughters. The Taylors' life changed completely when John was arrested (the nature of his crime is no longer known), convicted, and banished from England on a prison ship. Laura tried frantically to find out the ship's destination, but without success.

Needing to earn a living to support herself and her daughters, Laura was encouraged to try the stage. Her striking appearance and vivacious manner soon caught the eye of a prominent actress-manager, Madame Vestris. After a short period of coaching by Vestris, Laura made her acting debut with a touring theatrical troupe. She followed up the tour with an appearance in London, where her sparkling talent attracted the attention of an American actor-manager, James William Wallack. Laura was flattered when Wallack offered to bring her to America and readily accepted his invitation. She arrived in New York accompanied by her mother and two daughters, whom she introduced as her nieces. Laura didn't want anything to mar the youthful impression she hoped to make in America.

After a hugely successful run in New York, Keene embarked on a tour of the country, and now she was in San Francisco, performing with Edwin Booth. Unfortunately, the Bay city critics did not respond as enthusiastically to her charms as the reviewers in Eastern cities had. Laura blamed her cool reception on Edwin. To anyone who would listen, she said his youth—at twenty, he was seven years younger than she—and inexperience prevented him from giving her the proper support.

Edwin made light of her criticisms, joking to friends that he "felt them Keenely." Besides, he had something more important to think about. A well-known acting couple, Mr. and Mrs. James Stark, had recently returned to San Francisco with tales of the fortune they had amassed on a tour of Australia. The Starks' glowing account excited Edwin and gave him fresh hope. The wealth he'd expected to obtain in California had eluded him thus far, but who was to say he wouldn't find it in Australia?

Laura Keene responded with even greater enthusiasm to the possibility

Laura Keene as Portia in Shakespeare's *The Merchant of Venice.*
The Library of Congress

of an Australian tour. But her main reason for wanting to go was very different from Edwin's. Laura had never given up the search for her husband, John Taylor, and she thought she might locate him in Australia, the colony to which Britain shipped many of its criminals in the nineteenth century. Leaving her mother and her two daughters in San Francisco, Laura set sail for Australia in late July 1854 with Edwin, Dave Anderson, and the other members of the acting company.

The voyage took seventy-two days, eleven of which the passengers spent becalmed in the middle of the Pacific, waiting for a wind to propel the ship forward. It was October, the middle of the hot Australian spring, before they finally docked in Sydney harbor. After such a long trip, their disappointment was all the greater when they discovered that Australia was in the middle of an economic slump. They received good reviews in both Sydney and Melbourne, but audiences were sparse in the first city and even smaller in the second.

Once again Laura blamed Edwin for the poor attendance and tried to get him to spend more time rehearsing. He managed to escape from her on his twenty-first birthday, which he celebrated in Melbourne on November 13. First he went to a photographer's studio, where he had his picture taken. Then he and Dave Anderson made the rounds of the city's bars. Edwin drank until he got dizzy, then staggered back to his hotel, where he planted an American flag in the courtyard and shouted that the United States was a bigger and better country than Great Britain.

Neither Edwin nor Laura made any money to speak of on their ill-fated Australian tour. But Laura did at least discover what had happened to her husband. While in Melbourne, she learned that John Taylor was serving a lifetime prison sentence there, with no chance of parole. She sought permission to visit him, but her request was denied. Realizing more clearly than ever that she was on her own, Laura packed her costumes and set sail for San Francisco with Edwin and the rest of the company.

In February 1855, the ship made a stop at Honolulu in the Hawaiian Islands. On a walk through the town, Edwin and the other actors noticed a vacant theater, the Royal Hawaiian. They decided to interrupt their trip, rent the theater, and put on a series of plays. If they were lucky, they might be able to make up some of the losses they'd suffered in Australia and return to San Francisco with a little more money in their pockets.

Unfortunately, Laura Keene clashed with Edwin during rehearsals for *Richard III* and flounced out of the theater. The ship that had brought the troupe from Australia was still in the harbor, loading supplies. Laura boarded it and sailed for home, leaving the others behind to make do without her. That proved to be quite a problem. The only replacement Edwin could find to play her part, Lady Anne, was a former stagehand from the States—a bowlegged man with slightly crossed eyes.

As rehearsals proceeded, Edwin reminded himself that men had played all the women's roles when Shakespeare's plays were first performed. And the stagehand's bowlegs weren't visible when he put on Lady Anne's long-skirted costume. But the man was still no actor, and Edwin was afraid the Hawaiian audience would laugh him off the stage. They didn't, though. The crowd that filled the Royal Hawaiian Theater sat quietly throughout, and they applauded long and loud at the end.

The next night the troupe performed *Hamlet*. "I often wondered," Edwin wrote later, "at the popularity of my Hamlet with the native chiefs. They used to come night after night, squat on their haunches directly in front of the stage [the front of the auditorium had no seats], and listen to the play from beginning to end. Between the acts they would apparently talk it over in their native tongue, in the most animated manner, and then when the curtain rose again they would resume their attitudes and expressions of deep interest and remain until the end of the performance."

By the end of March, Edwin and his fellow actors were eager to return to California. They didn't have much money left after purchasing their schooner tickets, but the enthusiastic welcome they'd received in Honolulu had given their spirits a tremendous boost. Edwin and the others sailed into San Francisco Bay in late April, wiser if not richer after their adventures in Australia and Hawaii.

June met Edwin at the dock and took him to his house on Telegraph Hill. There they began to catch up on everything that had happened since they'd last been together. June had made a trip back east to visit their mother and see how she and their brothers and sisters were doing. He was concerned, he said, about Johnnie. Their younger brother had been in and out of several Maryland boarding schools, where he had made friends with the sons of some of the South's most prominent slave-owning families. He had also earned a reputation among the young ladies in the neighborhood for being the handsomest boy in whatever school he attended, and the best dancer. But he showed little interest in his studies and was only an average student at best.

What worried June most, though, was Johnnie's headstrong nature and his resistance to any form of discipline. Johnnie wouldn't listen when June urged him to go back to school. All he wanted to do was stay at Tudor Hall, Johnnie said, although he wasn't much help to his mother in running the place. As he once told his sister Asia, he thought of farming as "trying to starve respectably by torturing the barren earth." Even as a boy, Johnnie had dreams that went far beyond the fields and barns of Tudor Hall. "I must have fame, fame!" he confided to Asia.

While June was back in Maryland, he tried to get their mother to take a strong stand with Johnnie. She refused, fearing Johnnie would only resent it and become even harder to handle. She asked June to stop needling his younger brother, and June agreed. He didn't want to provoke any unpleasant scenes during his brief visit. But he was still worried about Johnnie, and shared his concerns with Edwin in the hope that he might have some suggestions for dealing with their difficult brother.

Edwin had already decided to return to the East, and what June said about Johnnie made him even more eager to do so. But he didn't want to return home with only an empty wallet to show for all the time he had spent in California and Australia—especially since June had told him their mother was having a hard time making ends meet on the farm. Instead, he accepted an offer to act in a series of plays in San Francisco, and followed it up with an engagement in Sacramento and another tour of the goldfield towns.

Sometimes he was "on," and gave an excellent performance that was praised by audience and reviewers alike. Other times, especially when he'd been drinking, he didn't seem to care and barely managed to get through the play. When the latter happened, the audience frequently booed, and reviewers criticized Edwin severely. After an especially sloppy performance in Sacramento of a play called *The Corsican Brothers*, the reviewer for the *Journal* wrote: "Mr. Booth, who was cast to sustain the principal character, could hardly sustain himself, but he struggled through the play, dragging everything down to the depths of disgust. Speaking mildly, he was intoxicated."

Back in Sacramento after the conclusion of the goldfields tour, Edwin met a wealthy patron of the theater, M. F. Butler, who admired the young actor's talent but hated the way he was misusing it. Butler urged Edwin to pull himself together and go back east, and he offered to organize two benefits to help speed Edwin on his way. Heartened by Butler's proposition, Edwin came through with one of his best performances in a play by the English writer Edward Bulwer-Lytton about Cardinal Richelieu of France.

Edwin *Booth*

From daguerratype taken 1856

Edwin Booth in 1856. *Shaw Collection, The Harvard Theatre Collection, Houghton Library*

He followed it up with an equally solid interpretation of the villainous Iago in Shakespeare's *Othello*.

The proceeds from these benefits enabled Edwin to pay off his debts but left him with little extra cash for the trip home. That problem was solved by a third benefit, this one in San Francisco. It was organized by twenty of the city's prominent businessmen and politicians, who said in a letter that they wanted to thank Edwin for the contributions he had made to the city's theatrical life.

Edwin was immensely gratified by their invitation and made plans to perform Shakespeare's *King Lear* for the first time. As in Sacramento, he disciplined himself and delivered a powerful performance. When the curtain fell at the end, he received a standing ovation. Gazing out at the audience, he smiled broadly and ripped off his long white wig and beard. The astonished crowd cheered even more loudly when they saw Edwin's boyish face. The actor who had moved them so deeply as the aged king was just twenty-two years old!

Two days later, Edwin stood on the deck of the steamer *The Golden Age* and waved good-bye to June as the vessel pulled away from the dock. It was September 5, 1856. Edwin had spent almost four years in California, with the side trip to Australia and Hawaii—four adventurous years during which he had experienced many of life's highs and lows, and had begun to discover his strengths as an actor. Now he was bound for home with $500 in his wallet, and once more he was traveling via the Isthmus of Panama. It wouldn't be the home he had left, though. There would be no father Junius to greet him with his booming voice and warnings not to harm any living thing.

His mother and brothers and sisters were sure to have changed greatly since he'd been away. In her letters, his mother always tried to put a good face on things, but he could tell she sorely missed his father. And he wondered if he'd recognize Johnnie. His younger brother had been a gangly boy when Edwin had left for California. Now he was on the verge of manhood, and something of a problem, according to June.

The country was changing, too, expanding westward at an ever more rapid rate. As it grew, the question of slavery acquired greater urgency. Until the 1850s, an uneasy balance had been maintained between the Southern states, where slavery was practiced, and the Northern states, where it was outlawed. But what about territories like Kansas and Nebraska that wanted to join the Union as new states? Kansas had earned the nickname "Bloody Kansas" when open warfare had broken out in 1855 between the proslavery forces and those who were determined the state would be free.

Edwin was probably not aware that this conflict was still raging as his ship steamed down along the Pacific coast of Mexico on its way to Panama. Then and later, he always said that he was not a political person. But he came from a slave state, Maryland, that lay on the dividing line between North and South. There was no way that Edwin and his family could avoid the clash of beliefs that was already threatening to tear the country apart.

Chapter 6
EDWIN IN LOVE

*E*VEN THOUGH HE'D EXPECTED to find them changed, Edwin was startled when he saw his family again. Gray streaked his mother's black hair, and deep creases had formed around her mouth. None of the tenant farmers she'd hired to run Tudor Hall had worked out, and the winters in the country were so severe that she and the girls longed to move to a more comfortable spot.

His sister Asia, whom Edwin remembered as a shy schoolgirl, had grown into a handsome young woman of twenty-one. She was being courted by, and would soon marry, John Sleeper Clarke, a boyhood friend of Edwin's from Baltimore. But the most changed of all was John Wilkes. The awkward boy of fourteen was now a confident young man of eighteen—and a spectacularly handsome one.

As for Edwin, "he seemed older in experience only" according to Asia. Writing about the family later, his sister said Edwin still looked like a boy when he came home, "and very fragile; his mild dark eyes and long locks gave him an air of melancholy. He had the gentle dignity and inherent grace that one attributes to a young prince."

Edwin was always shy at social gatherings. He often sat in a corner and spoke to no one, while his brother John flirted and danced with one young woman after another. Those who knew him well said that Edwin suffered stage fright everywhere except on the stage.

After a brief holiday, Edwin was eager to get back to work. He'd hoped to make his first appearance in either Boston or New York, both of which had a large number of theaters and critics whose influence was felt across the country. But theatrical managers in those cities were afraid to take a chance on a relative newcomer, even one who bore the famous name of Booth. So Edwin had to settle for a booking in Baltimore, his home city. He would open there on October 15 in the title role of *Hamlet*, and follow it up with *Richelieu* and *Richard III*.

As he prepared for his debut, Edwin looked through his father's old costumes, which his mother had kept carefully stored at Tudor Hall. Edwin was thinner than Junius, but he thought some of his father's old outfits might be altered so that he could wear them when he played Richard and Cardinal Richelieu.

His mother surprised him by refusing to let him have the garments. While Edwin was still away, John Wilkes—who had always been Mrs. Booth's favorite—had made his acting debut playing a supporting part in another Baltimore production of *Richard III*. Now John seemed determined to pursue a stage career of his own, and his mother wanted to support his ambition in every way she could. So, as she explained to Edwin, she was saving her husband's old costumes for her younger son.

Edwin was disappointed, but he found substitutes for the outfits and opened in *Hamlet* on schedule. The Baltimore reviewers praised his acting in it and the other plays in his repertory, and he concluded his two-week run with a successful benefit performance. The next stop on his Eastern tour was Richmond, Virginia, where he would open in *Richard III* and then play the male lead in Shakespeare's classic drama of young love, *Romeo and Juliet*.

The Richmond theater was managed by Joseph Jefferson, the popular actor famed for his portrayal of Rip Van Winkle. Jefferson and his wife had taken into their home a sixteen-year-old actress from Troy, New York, named Mary Devlin. Mary had started working in the theater at the age of fourteen, after her father lost all his money in a failed business venture. After seeing Mary perform, the Jeffersons invited her to live with them and brought her to Richmond to play the leading roles for young women in their acting company. It was only natural, then, that she was assigned to play Juliet to Edwin's Romeo.

Edwin had had a number of romantic flings while living in the West, but none of them had evolved into a serious relationship. In their wake, he swore to his friends that he would never marry an actress. But Mary Devlin's dark-eyed beauty, cheerful manner, and easy grace aroused feelings

Mary Devlin.
Evert Jansen Wendell Collection,
The Harvard Theatre Collection,
Houghton Library

in him that he hadn't experienced before. After playing opposite her in *Romeo and Juliet,* Edwin wrote his mother: "I have seen and acted with a young woman who has so impressed me that I could almost forget my vow never to marry an actress."

Mary's response to Edwin was even more enthusiastic. When the curtain fell on *Romeo and Juliet,* she told Joseph Jefferson, "He is the greatest actor I have ever known. I was inspired and could act forever with him!"

Jefferson was suspicious. He knew how fickle actors could be, and he didn't want Mary—who was like a daughter to him—to be hurt. But after Edwin gave Mary a beautiful turquoise bracelet, Jefferson realized the actor was seriously interested in his ward. And when Mary and Edwin came to him at the end of the week and asked his blessing on their friendship,

Jefferson slipped into the role of Friar Lawrence in *Romeo and Juliet* and gave the young lovers his benediction.

Edwin and Mary did not become engaged at the end of his Richmond engagement, however. Edwin had a long road tour ahead of him, during which he hoped to establish his acting reputation in the East. Only when he'd accomplished that would he feel ready to make a firm commitment to Mary. But he thought of her constantly as he traveled on to Charleston, South Carolina; Mobile, Alabama; New Orleans, Louisiana; and then farther west to St. Louis, Missouri.

As the tour progressed, Edwin became embarrassed by the way he was described on posters announcing his performances. He was particularly upset by a billboard he saw outside a theater in Chicago. It read: COME SEE EDWIN BOOTH, THE WORLD'S GREATEST ACTOR, THE INHERITOR OF HIS FATHER'S GENIUS! How could he ever live up to a description like that? When he moved on to Detroit, he asked the theater manager there to announce him as "simply Edwin Booth, nothing more."

Upon arriving at the theater the next afternoon, he was surprised to see a crowd of people gathered near the entrance. They were looking at a poster and chuckling to one another. Once Edwin read the words on the poster, he understood why. The theater manager had followed his instruction exactly—too exactly. The poster read: "ENGAGEMENT FOR ONE WEEK ONLY OF SIMPLE EDWIN BOOTH." (In those days, the word *simple*, when used this way, meant "slow-witted.")

Whatever the posters said, audiences in the Midwest responded warmly to Edwin wherever he performed, and reviewers commented favorably on his acting. Word of his success carried back east, and his manager was finally able to get him a Boston booking in April 1857. For his first appearance in Boston, Edwin chose to play the villainous Sir Giles Overreach in the classic English drama *A New Way to Pay Old Debts*. In doing so, he risked comparisons with his father, who had often played Sir Giles. But Edwin brought his own strengths to the part, and he stunned the audience with his realistic acting when Sir Giles goes mad at the end of the play.

The reviews confirmed that his risk had paid off. The critic for the *Boston Transcript* wrote: "Quite a triumph for young Booth. . . . It brought back the most vivid recollections of the fire, the vigor, the strong intellectuality which characterized the acting of his late, lamented father."

Responding to the reviews, Boston theatergoers flocked to see Edwin. Louisa May Alcott, who would later write *Little Women,* attended one of his performances and made note of it in her journal. "Saw young Booth in *Brutus,*" she wrote, "and liked him better than his father." Julia Ward Howe, poet and social reformer and author of "The Battle Hymn of the Republic," went with her husband to see Edwin in *Richelieu.* At the end of his first big scene, they turned to each other and whispered, "This is the real thing!"

Edwin was cheered by the enthusiasm of his Boston audiences. But it wasn't enough to keep him from going on an occasional binge, as he had so often done in California. His drinking worried his fellow actors. An old-timer who had been in the cast of *Richard III* when Edwin made his stage debut took him aside one night and said, "Now, Ted, there is for you in a stage career either a fortune and the leading roles or—a bottle of brandy. You must cast aside Bohemianism. Be Hamlet everywhere."

Edwin listened respectfully, but he wasn't yet ready to change his ways.

After the Boston engagement ended, Booth traveled on to New York for a month-long stay at the Metropolitan Theatre on lower Broadway. He groaned when he saw the posters hailing him as the SON OF THE GREAT TRAGEDIAN, HOPE OF THE LIVING DRAMA. But by now he was used to theater managers hoping to sell more tickets by emphasizing his connection to his famous father.

The New York reviews of his opening performance in *Richard III* were mostly favorable. The *New York Tribune* called his acting "tame" in some of the early scenes, but went on to say that in the later ones "all his tameness instantly vanishes. He renders these passages with a vigorous truthfulness which startles the audience into wild enthusiasm."

During his New York stay, two young men saw Edwin act for the first time and were tremendously impressed. One of them was William Winter, who was just beginning his career as a newspaper critic, and who would later become one of Edwin's best friends. Winter sensed that Edwin was trying to escape from the shadow of his father's reputation. "A famous son makes his father famous by reflection," Winter wrote. "But the service is rarely reciprocated." He saw great potential in Edwin but urged him to explore his roles more deeply. If he did, Winter predicted, he would "eclipse any name which has adorned the English-speaking stage within the memory of living man."

Edwin Booth with an
ornate pipe.
George Doane Wells Collection,
The Harvard Theatre Collection,
Houghton Library

37 UNION SQR. N. Y.

Edwin read Winter's comments and took them to heart. When he acted Richard III and other parts associated with his father, he gradually dropped many of Junius's stage tricks—the broad gestures and drawn-out pauses—that didn't seem natural when he, Edwin, performed them. In their place, he adopted a more restrained acting style while making sure that his voice still reached those sitting farthest from the stage. Edwin was never one to talk much about his acting methods. But later, when asked by a fellow actor, Otis Skinner, to compare his approach to his father's, he said, "I think I am a little quieter."

The other young man who saw Edwin perform in New York and became one of his greatest admirers was Adam Badeau. A freelance journalist, Badeau wrote Booth a fan letter calling his acting "the incarnation of passion and romance and poetry." Edwin, touched, agreed to meet Badeau, and this marked the beginning of a close and enduring friendship. Edwin admitted to Badeau that he felt intellectually inferior because he had never gone to high school, let alone college. Badeau responded by offering to serve as a kind of tutor to Edwin. He advised the young actor on books he should read, accompanied him to art museums, and introduced Booth to his writer friends.

As their friendship deepened, Edwin told Badeau things he'd never told anyone else, not even his brother June. When he was onstage, playing Hamlet or Iago or Richard III, Booth could easily express the full range of human emotions; but offstage he found it extremely difficult to express his own. He admitted to Badeau that he was often overcome by waves of depression and suffered through many sleepless nights. At those times, he told his friend, he often had "the feeling that evil is hanging over me, that I can't come to any good." It was then, he confided, that he had the strongest urge to escape his depression by going on a binge. After that, Badeau did his best to distract his friend when he sensed one of Edwin's dark moods coming on, but he was not always successful.

In March 1858, Edwin returned to Baltimore and renewed his friendship with Mary Devlin, who was now performing with a company in that city. Their time apart had only strengthened Edwin's feelings for Mary, and he proudly introduced her to his mother and his sisters. Mrs. Booth and Rosalie were charmed by the shy young actress, but Asia was not. She thought Mary was interested only in Edwin's money and position.

Confused by Asia's negative reaction to Mary, Edwin left Baltimore without becoming engaged. But he kept in close touch with Mary by mail as they went their separate ways. That fall Edwin was acting in New York when a letter arrived from Mary, who was performing in Boston. She had met a wealthy lawyer, she said, and he had asked her to marry him. Distraught, Edwin sank into one of his worst depressions and went on a colossal binge. "He became quite wild," Adam Badeau wrote, "and plunged into such dissipation that it was necessary to close his engagement at the theater."

When Mary heard what had happened, she made arrangements to leave Boston as soon as possible, and took a train to New York. She found Edwin in bed, recuperating from a hangover. He apologized for his behavior, saying he'd grown up too soon. "Before I was eighteen I was a drunkard," he confessed. Mary tried to reassure him by telling him she had no intention of accepting the Boston lawyer's proposal of marriage. When he heard that, Edwin forgot his earlier hesitations and asked her to marry him. Mary happily accepted, and also agreed to give up her acting career. The stage was no fit place for a wife, Edwin said.

Unfortunately, they could not be married at once because of Edwin's acting commitments. They announced their engagement, however, to all their relatives and friends. Edwin's mother welcomed the news, but Asia could not overcome her earlier doubts about Mary. Adam Badeau wasn't overjoyed, either; he feared that Edwin would not have much time for him after he was married. Of those close to Edwin, only his brother John wholeheartedly approved of the match.

While Edwin was building his reputation in the East, John had been busy laying the foundation for his own acting career. In the fall of 1857, he got a job with the Arch Street Theatre in Philadelphia, playing any small part that was assigned to him for a beginner's salary of just eight dollars a week. To avoid comparison with his famous father and older brother, he was billed as "Mr. J. B. Wilkes."

He acted with the Arch Street company for a full season and gained confidence with each part he played. But sometimes he was struck dumb by stage fright and couldn't remember his next line. That happened on the opening night of the historical play *Lucretia Borgia* in February 1858. John entered center stage, dressed as a fifteenth-century gentleman, and opened his mouth to speak. He was supposed to say, "Madame, I am Petruchio Pandolfo." Instead, he went blank and sputtered, "Madame, I am Pondolfio Pet—Pedolfio Pat—Pantuchio Ped—Dammit! Who am I?"

The audience burst into laughter, and John laughed with them. What else could he do?

His striking appearance helped him overcome such awkward moments. Although he was quite short—not much more than five feet six—he had his father's commanding presence. Women everywhere responded to his curly black hair, his flowing mustache, and especially his intense dark eyes.

Fellow actor John Ellsler described them vividly: "At all times his eyes were his striking features, but when his emotions were aroused they were like living jewels. Flames shot from them."

Actress Clara Morris summed up the effect John had on those around him: "At the theatre, . . . as the sunflowers turn upon their stalks to follow the beloved sun, so old and young, our faces smiling, turned to him."

After finishing the season in Philadelphia, John decided to return to the South. He signed a contract for the 1858–59 season with a theater in Richmond, Virginia, which was then the center of theatrical activity in the Southern states. The manager of the theater promised him better parts and raised his pay to twenty dollars a week—not bad in a time when most workers considered themselves fortunate to get one dollar a day.

The young John Wilkes Booth.
The National Archives

In October 1858, his brother Edwin came to Richmond for a week of performances. On the fifth he played Hamlet, and John was cast as Hamlet's friend Horatio. In their scenes together, Edwin let John have center stage, and at the end of the play, he led his brother down to the footlights and said, "I think he's done well, don't you?" The audience shouted, "Yes! Yes!" and applauded loudly.

Privately, Edwin was less enthusiastic about John's abilities. "I don't think John will startle the world," he wrote in a letter to June. "But he is improving fast and looks beautiful onstage."

John was much happier in Richmond than he had been in Philadelphia, and in the spring of 1859 he signed on for another season with the Richmond Theatre. There were several reasons why he felt more at home in Virginia. Southern society was more accepting of actors than Northern society, which tended to think of theater people as shady and immoral. Along with his fellow actors, John was welcomed into some of Richmond's finest homes, where he danced with the daughters of the city's most prominent families.

John—unlike Edwin—had always leaned more toward the South than the North, and living in Richmond only strengthened this inclination. He told his sister Asia that he wanted "to be loved of the Southern people above all things." He would, he said, work hard to make himself "essentially a Southern actor."

Booth's identification with the South showed itself most strongly when the white antislavery leader John Brown was condemned to death in the fall of 1859. Brown had long been one of the nation's most ardent abolitionists—those who fought to abolish slavery throughout the United States. While living in Pennsylvania, Brown had helped a number of slaves escape to freedom via the Underground Railroad. Later, after moving to Kansas, he had sided with those who wanted the new state to be free and had led an attack on a proslavery settlement that resulted in the deaths of five men.

John Brown's exploits made him an abolitionist hero, and in 1858 he set in motion a scheme that he hoped would result in a major slave revolt. With the aid of his five sons and a small army of followers, he planned to establish a military stronghold in northern Virginia. It would be a safe haven to which escaping slaves could flee, and from which slave uprisings could be launched. As a first step, Brown rented a farm near Harpers Ferry,

Engraving of John Brown. *The National Archives*

Virginia, and collected an assortment of weapons. Then, on October 16, 1859, he and his troops attacked and occupied the federal arsenal in Harpers Ferry.

That was as far as Brown's scheme got. A Virginia militia force under the command of Colonel Robert E. Lee quickly surrounded the arsenal and recaptured it after a fierce struggle. Ten of Brown's followers were killed in the fighting, and he himself was wounded and captured. When news of Brown's arrest spread, he became a bigger hero than ever in the North. Southerners, on the other hand, denounced him as an archcriminal. Brought to a speedy trial, he was convicted of treason and sentenced to death by hanging.

It was at this point that John Wilkes Booth entered the story. One afternoon in late November, he stepped outside the Richmond Theatre during a rehearsal break and saw volunteers from the city's elite militia unit, the Grays, lining up across the street. They were about to board a special train that would take them to Charles Town, where John Brown was being held to await his execution. The authorities feared that Brown's supporters might try to organize an escape. The militia would stand guard day and night outside the prison to make sure that didn't happen.

John had been outraged when he read of Brown's attempt to foment a slave uprising, and he longed for a way to express his feelings. Now he saw his chance. Impulsively, he approached the leader of the militia and asked to be allowed to join the unit. The man was reluctant at first, but John's plea was so convincing that he gave in at last and issued the actor a uniform.

While John changed into the outfit, one of his friends asked him how the theater was going to get along without him. "I don't know, and I don't care!" John shouted as he ran to board the militia train.

Chapter 7
MARCHING OFF TO WAR

THE TROOP TRAIN was so crowded that John, unable to squeeze onto a coach, had to ride much of the way in the baggage car. At Charles Town, the militiamen were housed in an abandoned tin factory and slept on thin pallets of straw. But John and the others were in high spirits as they took up their patrol duties.

The evenings when he wasn't on guard, John entertained his fellow soldiers with readings from Shakespeare. One evening a reporter from a Richmond newspaper sat in on John's performance. The next day he wrote, "Amongst them [the soldiers] I notice Mr. J. Wilkes Booth, a son of Junius Brutus Booth, who, though not a member [of the troop], as soon as he heard the trap of the drum, threw down the sock and buskin [his job as an actor], and shouldered his musket with the Grays to the scene of deadly conflict."

When Edwin heard about John's impulsive action, he wrote his fiancée, Mary Devlin. "Your news concerning the mad step John has taken I confess does not surprise me," she replied. "'Tis a great pity he had not more sense but time will teach him. . . . I hope nothing serious will occur there [Charles Town], for it would frighten your mother so."

The hanging of John Brown was set for December 2, 1859. On that morning, the militiamen lined up in rows around the scaffold. John watched as Brown mounted the platform, a calm expression on his bearded face. The militiamen had their guns at the ready, but none of Brown's supporters attempted to disrupt the proceedings. John was glad to be part of such a historic event until the trap door beneath Brown opened and he swung back and forth in midair, dangling from the rope around his neck.

The hanging of John Brown. *Engraving from* Frank Leslie's Illustrated Newspaper.
The Library of Congress

Then John felt faint. He turned to the soldier standing next to him and asked if the man had a flask; he said he could use a good, stiff drink.

As a supporter of the South and all it stood for, John firmly believed that Brown had got his due. At the same time, he couldn't help but be impressed by the courageous way that Brown had met his death. Later, he told Asia, "He was a brave old man; his heart must have broken when he felt himself deserted."

Returning to Richmond after the execution, John was fired by the theater manager for leaving his job without giving any notice. But a large group of his fellow militiamen marched to the theater and persuaded the manager to take him back. Many Richmond theatergoers also wrote letters to the manager in support of John. All the publicity about his having run off to join the militia had only increased his fame and popularity.

John finished out the 1859–60 season in Richmond while Edwin continued his tour of Eastern cities. Mary, who was now studying music in New York, wrote Edwin faithfully. Often she expressed how much he meant to her: "My spirit ever seems lighter and more joyous when I'm with you. This I can account for only by believing that a mission has been given me to fulfil, and that I shall be rewarded by seeing you rise to be great and happy." But she realized she would always have to share him with the theater. "If my love is selfish, you will never be great," she wrote. "Part of you belongs to the world. I *must* remember this."

Edwin and Mary were married in New York on July 7, 1860. Edwin's friend Adam Badeau attended the ceremony, which was held in the home of the Episcopal clergyman who presided. Also present were Mary's sister and Edwin's brother John, who had traveled up from Richmond for the occasion. Afterward, the newlyweds went on a honeymoon trip to Niagara Falls, accompanied by Edwin's mother and younger brother Joseph. Later, Adam Badeau joined the group at the Falls. Asia would have nothing to do with the wedding or the honeymoon; she still could not bring herself to accept Mary.

That fall, Edwin and Mary rented an apartment at the Fifth Avenue Hotel in New York, and he embarked on an extended season at the city's Winter Garden theater. John, his reputation enhanced by his success in Richmond, was engaged to go on tour for the first time as a star actor. He would play leading roles at theaters in Columbus, Georgia, and Montgomery, Alabama, and would receive a share of each night's box-office receipts. As a company member in Richmond, he had earned twenty dollars a week; now, if he appeared in a popular play, he could make several hundred or even a thousand dollars for each performance.

While Edwin was acting in New York and John was performing in the South, the United States was entering one of the tensest periods in its history. The presidential election of 1860 brought to a head the growing conflict between North and South. The Democratic party, reflecting the conflict, split in two. The Southern branch nominated its own candidate for president, John C. Breckinridge, who stood for states' rights, including the right to own slaves. Northern Democrats reacted by nominating as their candidate Stephen Douglas, who argued that the Union must be preserved at all costs but hoped that a compromise might still be achieved on the slavery issue.

The newly formed Republican party chose Abraham Lincoln as its candidate. Lincoln, like Douglas, was a strong advocate for the preservation of the Union; he once said, "A house divided against itself cannot stand." Unlike Douglas, however, he considered slavery both unjust and immoral, and was utterly opposed to its extension. His position on slavery earned him the support of Northern abolitionists, even though Lincoln was not an abolitionist himself. But it earned him the enmity of several Southern states, including South Carolina, which threatened to withdraw from the Union if he were elected president. These threats were put to the test in November 1860, when Lincoln won the hotly contested four-way election. (The fourth candidate was John Bell of the small Constitutional Union Party.)

Edwin Booth later confessed to a friend that, busy with his own affairs, he hadn't taken the trouble to vote. It's not known whether John Wilkes Booth voted. If he did go to the polls, he certainly didn't cast his ballot for Abraham Lincoln, a man whose views he despised. Besides, John had another, more pressing problem to deal with. On October 16, toward the end of his engagement in Georgia, Booth was accidentally shot in the thigh by his manager, Matthew Canning. The two men were backstage, inspecting Canning's new pistol, when the gun went off. Although it was just a flesh wound, Booth did not return to the stage until October 29; by then the company had moved on to Montgomery, Alabama.

The wound was still troubling John when the Montgomery run ended, so he decided to go to his mother's home to recuperate further. Mrs. Booth and Rosalie were now living in Philadelphia, near the recently married Asia. On December 13, a "Grand Union Demonstration" attended by more than 10,000 Philadelphians took place in a square near Independence Hall. John may have been among those listening as speaker after speaker rose to condemn Northern extremists for driving the Southern states out of the Union. Philadelphia merchants conducted a great deal of trade with the South and they feared their businesses would suffer if the Union split apart. In the end, the rally's leaders pushed through resolutions urging strict enforcement of the Fugitive Slave Laws, under which any slave caught fleeing to the North could be forcibly returned to the South, and the opening up of federal territories in the Midwest to slavery.

Whether John attended the rally or not, he no doubt read about it in the Philadelphia newspapers. Clearly he was influenced by its resolutions when, later in December, he drafted a speech expressing his own fervent support for the South. The speech was never finished, let alone delivered, but it reveals the depth of John's feelings. "You all feel the fire now raging in the nation's heart," he wrote. "It is a fire lighted and fanned by Northern fanaticism. A fire which naught but blood & justice can extinguish. I tell you the Abolitionist doctrine is the fire which, if allowed to rage, will consume the house and crush us all beneath its ruins."

John Wilkes Booth as a successful young actor.
The Library of Congress

Booth argued that the rights of Southerners to own slaves and pursue their traditional way of life must be respected. Otherwise, he warned, South Carolina and eventually "the whole South" would secede from the Union. "Fierce Civil War will follow. And then, what then? *Why God alone can tell the rest,*" he concluded. Unfortunately, events had progressed too rapidly for warnings like Booth's to have any effect. Outraged by the election of Abraham Lincoln, South Carolina did not even wait until he had been inaugurated before making its move. It seceded from the Union on December 20, 1860, and six other Deep South states—Georgia, Florida, Alabama, Mississippi, Louisiana, and Texas—quickly followed suit.

John must have been deeply disappointed by these developments, but he didn't let them keep him from pursuing his career. He signed on for a tour of Northern cities in the spring of 1861, starting with an engagement in Rochester, New York. Meanwhile, a last attempt at a compromise in the U.S. Congress between the Northern and Southern positions on slavery failed, and in February 1861, Jefferson Davis was inaugurated as president of the seven rebel Confederate States of America.

At the time of Davis's inauguration, Abraham Lincoln was riding across the country by special train from his home in Illinois, heading toward *his* inauguration in Washington, D.C. Lincoln's train made a stop in Albany, New York, where John Wilkes Booth was performing in a series of plays. It is not known if Booth was in the huge crowd that greeted Lincoln in Albany, straining for a glimpse of the tall, gaunt president-elect. But many people in the hotel where Booth was staying heard John loudly denounce Lincoln and proclaim his own solidarity with the South. The actor's outbursts offended the other guests, some of whom complained to the manager of the theater where Booth was appearing. The manager took Booth aside, telling him he'd better watch what he said. Otherwise, he risked being booed off the stage or worse.

John Wilkes was outraged. "Is not this a democratic city?" he exclaimed.

"Democratic, yes, but disunion, no!" the manager replied. His rebuke silenced Booth—for the moment.

Abraham Lincoln was inaugurated on March 4, 1861, and less than two weeks later he faced his first major crisis as president. Ever since South Carolina had seceded from the Union, its governor had been demanding that control of all federal property in the state be handed over to him. That property included Fort Sumter, located in the harbor of the city of Charleston.

In his campaign for president, Lincoln had pledged to defend every piece of federal property in the South. Now, just as South Carolina's governor was stepping up pressure on Fort Sumter, Lincoln learned that its garrison—which was loyal to the Union—was running out of supplies. If he sent the necessary provisions, the president knew, the convoy might be attacked, and war would almost certainly follow. But if he didn't, the garrison would face either slow starvation or a humiliating surrender.

After weighing his options, the president decided to dispatch a fleet of supply ships to Charleston, and he notified the governor of South Carolina that it was on its way. The governor responded to the president's message by demanding that the commander of the fort evacuate it at once. When the commander refused, Southern guns opened up on Fort Sumter early in the morning of April 12, 1861, and the fort's guns returned the fire. The American Civil War had begun.

President Lincoln immediately called for the mobilization of an army of volunteers to fight the forces of the seven Confederate states. His call became even more urgent when four additional Southern states—Arkansas, North Carolina, Virginia, and Tennessee—joined the Confederacy. All across the North, eager young men rushed to enlist in the Union army. In New York, new recruits drilled in the city's parks and paraded along Broadway while crowds of excited onlookers sang "The Star-Spangled Banner."

Edwin's close friend Adam Badeau was among those who enlisted, but Edwin himself resisted the call. Preoccupied with his career and his new wife, he chose to finish his season at New York's Winter Garden theater. Rarely had he seen larger or more enthusiastic audiences. Along with the city's residents, the theaters were crowded with military men and out-of-town businesspeople, all of them eager to escape the tension and anxiety caused by the war. One regular theatergoer, Mrs. John Sherwood, expressed the general mood in her diary: "In that first year of the war, when we were profoundly miserable and frightened, what a relief it was to go and see Edwin Booth in *Hamlet*."

No one ever thought that John Wilkes would enlist in the Union army. But many who knew his political leanings wondered why he didn't return

Confederate guns bombard Fort Sumter. *The Library of Congress*

to his beloved South and join the ranks of the Confederacy. Years later, Edwin remembered a conversation he had had with his younger brother. "I asked him once why he did not join the Confederate Army," Edwin wrote to an inquiring historian. "To which he replied: 'I promised Mother I would keep out of the quarrel, if possible, and am sorry that I said so.'"

When the war broke out, John had just returned to Albany, New York, for a second round of appearances. He found the city draped in Union flags to protest the South's firing on Fort Sumter. This set John off. To anyone who would listen, he proclaimed his admiration for the South's soldiers and called their action the most heroic of modern times. Such utterances did not sit well with many of the Northerners who heard them. Union sympathizers urged that John be banned from the stage as long as he continued to make what they called "treasonable statements." Others came to John's defense, citing his superior gifts as an actor and claiming that they had never heard him denounce the North except when he had had too much to drink.

His supporters won the day, and John continued to perform, earning rave reviews from the Albany drama critics. One critic wrote: "Mr. Booth is full of genius, and this with his fine face and figure, and his artistic conceptions of the characters he performs, will always render him a favorite."

John may have been a favorite of Albany audiences, but he made an enemy in that city who almost cost him his life. Earlier, he had embarked on an affair with Henrietta Irving, the talented and temperamental actress who was his leading lady on the northern tour. On their return to Albany, Miss Irving suspected that he had switched his affections to another young woman. Consumed with jealousy, she confronted John at a party in their hotel, pulled a dagger from her purse, and tried to stab him in the heart.

John threw up his arms to ward off the blow and escaped with a superficial scratch across his face. Miss Irving did not wait to see what had happened. Thinking she had killed Booth, she rushed to her room and stabbed herself. Fortunately, the wound was not serious and she survived. John, grateful to have been spared and perhaps feeling guilty, did not press charges against her. When the engagement in Albany was over, he packed his theatrical trunk and went once again to his mother's house in Philadelphia to rest and recuperate.

As spring turned into summer, both the North and the South continued to mobilize for all-out war. The North had certain definite advantages in the contest. It was composed of twenty-three states with a population of more than 22 million, whereas the South was made up of just eleven states with about 9 million people, nearly 4 million of whom were slaves. The North also possessed most of the factories needed to produce guns and ammunition, along with a much more extensive network of railroads than the South and a far larger and more powerful navy. For its part, the South had more trained military men at its disposal, beginning with its president, Jefferson Davis, who was a graduate of West Point.

Because of their region's advantages, many in the North thought the war would be over quickly. Acting on that assumption, President Lincoln and his generals launched an invasion of Virginia in July 1861. Their goal was to sweep across the state, vanquish all opposing forces, and seize

President Abraham Lincoln. *Photo by Alexander Gardner. The Library of Congress*

Richmond, the capital of the Confederacy. The Northerners were so sure that victory would be theirs that flocks of government officials and other residents of Washington, D.C., followed the Union army into Virginia. They brought along picnic baskets, blankets to spread on the ground, and binoculars through which they planned to watch the fighting.

Soldiers and spectators alike were in for a rude shock. On July 21, the Union army, made up largely of ill-trained volunteers, met a superior Confederate force at Bull Run, a small stream thirty miles southwest of Washington. Both sides fought bravely, but the Union soldiers were no match for their more experienced Southern counterparts. After suffering heavy casualties, the Northerners broke ranks and retreated toward Washington along roads jammed with panicky civilians, their picnic plans forgotten.

The Battle of Bull Run made it clear that the war would be a long, hard struggle. There's no record of how John Wilkes Booth reacted to news of the Confederate victory, but he must have been overjoyed. Edwin, who was spending the summer in New York, had a more personal reason to be happy. He had long wanted to perform in England, his parents' homeland, and now an invitation had come to act that fall at the Haymarket Theatre in London. "It is the grand turning-point of my career," he wrote to a New York friend, Richard Cary, who was serving as a captain in the Union army.

Then Edwin realized that he had been writing "I, I, I," throughout the letter with no thought to what Cary, in the thick of the war, might be feeling. He apologized for his insensitivity and concluded: "God bless you, my boy! And stick to the flag, Dick, as I intend to do, though far away."

Edwin and his wife, Mary, sailed for England in late August and arrived in good time for him to prepare for his London debut at the Haymarket on September 30. Mary, whose health was frail, had her own preparations to make. She was expecting a child in December and was determined that nothing should go wrong.

Chapter 8
"HE MUST COME AT ONCE"

*E*DWIN'S LONDON DEBUT was not the great success he had hoped for. In fact, it came close to being an outright failure. Most of the English actors in his supporting cast at the Haymarket Theatre adopted a superior attitude toward Edwin, and this made him lose confidence onstage. As a result, the reviews of his performances in *The Merchant of Venice* and *Richard III* were decidedly cool.

The manager of the Haymarket didn't help matters by spending as little as possible on sets and costumes. In *Richard III*, the extras' tin armor was so heavy and poorly constructed that one actor who knelt before the king, played by Edwin, couldn't get up again without help. Another extra barely managed to yank his arm back down after raising it in a salute. Only when he played the cardinal in *Richelieu* did Edwin overcome the obstacles in his way and win over both the London audience and the city's influential critics.

After concluding his season in the British capital, Edwin went on a tour of the provinces. But his reception in Manchester and Liverpool was no better than it had been at first in London. Complicating matters was the fact that many people in Great Britain sided with the Confederacy in the American Civil War because they believed the Southerners were more in tune with their own aristocratic ideas. Edwin wrote Adam Badeau that he had given up reading the pro-South *Times* of London because it was "so rabid against us."

When his provincial tour ended, Edwin rushed back to London to be with Mary when their child was born. To show his support for his war-torn homeland, Edwin obtained an American flag and hung it like a canopy over Mary's bed, thus making sure in his own way that their child would be born under the Stars and Stripes. The baby arrived a few hours later, on December 9, 1861. "A daughter," Edwin cabled a friend in America, "and thank God, all is well with her and her mother." The proud parents named the little girl Edwina, after her father.

Edwin did no more acting in England. Instead, he devoted himself to helping Mary recover her strength. By the spring of 1862, she was well enough to travel, and he took her and baby Edwina on a trip to Paris. After hiring a French nanny for their little daughter, Edwin and Mary went sightseeing, and he delighted in buying his wife a wardrobe of stylish Paris gowns. Later that spring, the Booths returned to England, accompanied by the nanny, and then in August they all sailed for New York.

While he was abroad, and especially when he was in Paris, Edwin could probably forget at times that the Civil War was raging back home. But soon

Mary Devlin Booth with her infant daughter, Edwina.
The Museum of the City of New York, gift of Miss Florence Magonigle

after arriving in New York, he was reminded of the conflict in a sharply personal way. Word came that his friend Richard Cary had been killed during the fierce fighting at Antietam in northwestern Maryland. Antietam would come to be known as one of the bloodiest battles in the entire war, with 12,000 dead and wounded on the Union side and almost the same number of Confederate casualties.

"Dick was a hero born," Edwin wrote to Richard Cary's sister, and several days later, still grief stricken, he wrote another letter to his friend Adam Badeau, who was still serving with the Union army. "To talk about such old-time nonsense as my own affairs is now too trivial," he said. "May the God of Battles guard you, Ad."

Despite the staggering death toll at Antietam, it was counted as a Union victory because Northern troops drove General Robert E. Lee's Confederate army back into Virginia. President Lincoln made the victory the occasion for issuing the Emancipation Proclamation on September 22, 1862. The Proclamation, which was to take effect in January 1863, granted freedom to all the slaves residing in the eleven states of the Confederacy. However, it did not free those slaves living in the border states of Delaware, Maryland, Kentucky, and Missouri, which had remained loyal to the Union.

President Lincoln's own views were not reflected in the Emancipation Proclamation. He favored a more gradual freeing of the slaves, to be undertaken voluntarily by the states and with federal payments to the slaveholders to compensate them for their losses. Lincoln thought such a plan only just since, in his view, the North was as responsible as the South for the existence of slavery in America. But he realized the Emancipation Proclamation was a political necessity if he was to continue to have the backing of antislavery Northerners who had helped vote him into office.

It is not known how Edwin Booth reacted to the news of the Emancipation Proclamation. Nor was the reaction of his brother John recorded. During the year that Edwin was in England and France, John continued to perform mainly in the North, with a few engagements in border states such as Missouri and Maryland. Audiences from St. Louis to Cleveland to New York loved the way John hurled himself into his roles. But his freewheeling style could be hard on his fellow performers.

In her memoirs, actress Kate Reignolds recalled what it was like to act with John. "He was as undisciplined on the stage as off," she wrote. "How he threw me about! In the last scene of *Romeo and Juliet* one night, I vividly recall how the buttons on his cuff caught my hair, and in trying to tear them out he trod on my dress and rent [tore] it so as to make it utterly useless afterward; and in his last struggle he literally shook me out of my shoes! The curtain fell on Romeo with a sprained thumb, a good deal of hair on his sleeve, Juliet in rags and two white satin shoes lying in the corner of the stage!"

Reignolds offered a shrewd appraisal of John as a person as well as a performer. "He was ever spoiled and petted, and left to his unrestrained will," she wrote. "The stage door was always blocked with silly women waiting to catch a glimpse, as he passed, of his superb face and figure. . . . He succeeded in gaining position by flashes of genius, but the necessity of ordinary study had not been borne in on him."

Her view of John's limitations was echoed in the comment of a Boston drama critic in 1862. After seeing Booth in a variety of roles, the critic wrote: "We have been greatly pleased, and greatly disappointed. . . . In what does he fail? Principally, in knowledge of himself—of his resources, how to husband and how to use them. . . . He ignores the fundamental principle of all vocal study and exercise: that the chest, and not the throat or mouth, should supply the sound necessary for singing or speaking." The critic warned that John was in danger of ruining his voice if he didn't learn how to use it correctly.

For now, though, John was content to accept one starring engagement after another and revel in the money he was making. "My goose does indeed hang high (long may she wave)," he wrote a friend in the fall of 1862. "I have picked up on an average this season over $650 per week. My first week here [Chicago] paid me near $900. And this week has opened even better."

As John's income grew, he invested heavily in the costumes he wore for the various roles he played. The costume trunk that he shipped from city to city on his tours was filled with velvet jackets, fur-trimmed robes, silk shirts, wool and cotton tights, wigs, slippers, and knee-high leather boots. John spent lavishly on his personal wardrobe too. No one could fail to admire his wealth and taste as he strode along city streets dressed in a wine-colored jacket and dove-gray trousers, a broad-brimmed hat set rakishly on his head.

Playbill for Shakespeare's *Romeo and Juliet* with John Wilkes
Booth as Romeo and Kate Reignolds as Juliet.
The Harvard Theatre Collection, Houghton Library

John Wilkes Booth in one
of his stylish outfits.
The Library of Congress

While John was happily touring, Edwin and Mary and little Edwina were settling into a suite of rooms at New York's Fifth Avenue Hotel. After the European trip, Edwin was tired of traveling, and he planned to limit his appearances in the 1862–63 season to New York and Boston primarily. "Starring around the country is sad work," he wrote his friend and fellow actor Lawrence Barrett, and it was made doubly difficult by the war. Besides, he wanted to spend more time with his wife and baby daughter.

Staying in one place presented its own problems, however. In New York, where he was playing an extended engagement at the Winter Garden, Edwin and Mary found themselves caught up in a social whirl. Midnight suppers after the play in the company of artists like Launt Thompson and Albert Bierstadt, and writers like Richard Henry Stoddard and Thomas

Bailey Aldrich, became an almost nightly occurrence. To overcome his natural shyness, Edwin began to drink again, occasionally at first and then more frequently. One glass of wine would lead to another, and then another. More than one morning, Mary would have to tell callers, "Alas, Mr. Booth is not well today."

In November 1862, Edwin was due to begin a month-long engagement in Boston. Lately, Mary had been suffering from headaches and a constant feeling of fatigue. Fearing that her lungs might become infected, her doctor recommended that she spend the winter months in some quiet locale where she could rest and regain her strength. New York, with its hectic pace, was not the place for that, so the Booths decided to rent a house for the winter in the town of Dorchester, just outside Boston. Mary would be able to see a local physician who specialized in cases like hers, and Edwin could use the house as a base during his Boston engagement.

Critics and audiences alike gave Booth a tremendous welcome in Boston that November. "Edwin has made nearly $5000 in just the first two weeks!" Mary wrote joyfully to a friend in New York. Then, in January, John came to Boston to star in a season of plays at the Boston Museum. He was greeted even more enthusiastically, if such a thing were possible. "Extraordinary!" is how the reviewer from the *Boston Transcript* described his acting.

Edwin rode in from Dorchester with Mary to see his brother perform the leading role in a popular melodrama titled *The Apostate*. Later, Edwin was full of praise for John's performance. "He played Pescara, a bloody villain of the deepest red, and he presented him—not underdone but rare enough for the most fastidious beef-eater," Edwin wrote to his New York friend Richard Stoddard. If Edwin was at all envious of his brother, he certainly didn't show it. "I am happy to state that he is full of the true grit . . . and when time and study round his rough edges he'll bid them all [the acting competition] 'stand apart!'"

During John's engagement, a critic for the *Boston Post* offered an interesting comparison of his and Edwin's acting: "Edwin has more poetry; John Wilkes more passion; Edwin has more melody of movement and utterance, John Wilkes more energy and animation; Edwin is more correct, John Wilkes more spontaneous; Edwin is more Shakespearean, John Wilkes more melodramatic; and in a word Edwin is a better Hamlet, John Wilkes a better Richard III."

When he had a day off, John enjoyed visiting Edwin and Mary in Dorchester and getting to know his niece, Edwina. But the brothers were careful not to discuss politics or President Lincoln or the progress of the war. They held such contrary views on these issues that both knew any discussion was likely to end in an angry argument or worse.

In February, Edwin was set to play a return engagement at the Winter Garden in New York. Mary wanted to go to New York with him, but Edwin felt it would be better if she stayed on in Dorchester, as her doctor had recommended. At last Mary gave in, but she asked their mutual friends in New York to keep a close eye on Booth. She was concerned that her beloved Edwin might resume his heavy drinking if left alone.

At first Mary's worries seemed groundless. Edwin opened his New York season in *Hamlet*, and the *New York Times* noted that "he played excellently to a house overflowing with one of those peculiarly fashionable and intelligent audiences" that Booth always attracted. But within a few days he seemed to lose his grip. It was obvious that he was drinking again. He lurched uncertainly around the stage, his voice loud one moment, then so soft that it could barely be heard.

His friends did their best to keep him in line. One evening in Booth's ground-floor dressing room, Thomas Bailey Aldrich snatched a glass of liquor away from the actor's valet before Booth could get it, and emptied the glass out an open window into the alley. Another time Aldrich and Richard Stoddard followed Booth for hours after a performance and kept him from entering any of the bars he passed, much as Booth himself had once trailed his wayward father.

The friends' efforts were not always successful, however, and the reviewers were the first to take notice. "Seldom have we seen Shakespeare so murdered as at the Winter Garden during the past two weeks," wrote the critic of the *New York Herald*. "It would have been better to disappoint the public by closing the theater than to place Mr. Booth upon the stage when he was really unfit to act."

At last Elizabeth Stoddard, Richard's wife, wrote to Mary, telling her what was going on and urging her to come to New York. "Sick or well, you must come," Mrs. Stoddard said. "Mr. Booth has lost all restraint and hold on himself. Last night there was the grave question of ringing down the curtain before the performance was half over."

Unfortunately, Mary was in no shape to make the trip. She had come down with a bad cold that in a few days had developed into pneumonia. She hadn't informed Edwin because she didn't want him to be anxious or interrupt his New York season. But she could no longer deny the truth of her condition. "I cannot come. I cannot stand," she replied to Elizabeth Stoddard. "I am going to try to write to him now, and God give me grace to write as a true wife should."

That evening, before she could compose the letter, Mary's illness took a drastic turn for the worse. Alarmed, her doctor sent off an urgent telegram to Edwin at the Winter Garden. When he got no answer, he sent a second telegram, and then a third. Meanwhile, a drunken Edwin was staggering through a performance of *Richard III*. Just after the final curtain came down, the theater manager hurried into the actor's dressing room with yet another telegram from Mary's doctor, this one addressed to the manager. "Why does not Mr. Booth answer? He must come at once," the doctor wrote. Mary was near death.

The doctor's blunt words shook Edwin out of his stupor. Only then did he open the three other telegrams and realize just how ill Mary was. Filled with guilt, he prepared to leave for the railroad station but was told the last train to Boston had already departed. After sending word to Mary's doctor that her husband would be on the first train in the morning, Richard Stoddard persuaded Edwin to accompany him to his apartment.

As the night wore on, no one thought of sleep. Elizabeth Stoddard gave Edwin cup after cup of black coffee while the actor paced back and forth. "Like a zoo animal in a cage," Mrs. Stoddard recalled later. Occasionally he would stop pacing, twist his hands, and turn haunted eyes from one of his hosts to the other. He could talk only of Mary—how much she had given him, and how much he loved her. One minute he refused to believe she was as ill as the doctor had said, the next he acted as if she were already dead, and gave in to racking sobs.

At last dawn came, and he and Richard Stoddard left for the railroad station. There Edwin took time to send a telegram that said simply, "Mary, I'm coming." Then he and Stoddard climbed aboard the seven-o'clock train for Boston.

Chapter 9
A SPY AND
A BLOCKADE RUNNER

THE WINTRY SKY was still dark as the train sped north. Later, Edwin would write his friend Adam Badeau that "I saw every time I looked from the window Mary dead, with a white cloth tied around her neck and chin. I saw her distinctly, a dozen times at least."

At Back Bay Station in Boston, a friend waited with a carriage to take Edwin and Richard Stoddard to Dorchester. Before the man could utter a word, Edwin raised a hand and said, "Do not tell me. I know." He climbed into the carriage with the others, and the three of them rode in silence through the streets of the city.

As soon as the carriage stopped in front of his house, Edwin dropped down from it and raced inside. He took the stairs two at a time and entered Mary's room. She lay on the bed with a white cloth tied around her neck and chin for warmth, just as Edwin had visualized her when he'd looked out the train window. And she was dead, as he had feared. The doctor told Edwin she had breathed her last a little after seven.

Edwin asked to be left alone with her body. He sat by her bed for hours, and when he finally emerged, he said nothing to anyone. But Stoddard noticed that he had taken a single rose from a bouquet on the table and placed it between Mary's hands. Around her neck he had hung a chain with a locket containing a miniature portrait of himself.

Later, in a letter to Adam Badeau, Edwin gave vent to his feelings. "One week's illness," he wrote. "Can you believe it, Ad? I can't." He was filled with remorse. "Had she had cheering news from me, or of me, it would have given her strength to rally. My conduct hastened her death, and when she

Edwin Booth in the 1860s, around the time of the death of his first wife, Mary.
The Harvard Theatre Collection, Houghton Library

heard that I—her all—was lost to all sense of decency and respect for her— her feeble spirit sank."

He regretted all the times when "cold, indifferent, like a statue I received her deep devotion. . . . Although my love was deep-rooted in my soul yet I could never *show* it. . . . If I were a poet I could tell you how I loved my Mary, but as it is I can only say I loved and let you guess how deeply."

The funeral service took place at Mount Auburn Cemetery in nearby Cambridge. Edwin's brother John Wilkes made a point of being there to lend Edwin his support. So did Edwin's mother, Mary Ann, and his brother-in-law, John Sleeper Clarke, both of whom had come up from Philadelphia. But Asia did not attend; she still had not gotten over her aversion to Mary.

Julia Ward Howe, the Boston writer who had long admired Edwin and who had gotten to know Mary, too, was also present at the service. In her diary, she wrote, "As Edwin Booth followed the casket, his eyes heavy with grief, I could not but remember how often I had seen him act the part of Hamlet at the stage burial of Ophelia." Mrs. Howe filed past Mary's open casket and later observed: "Hers was a most pathetic figure as she lay, serene and lovely, surrounded with flowers."

The weeks passed, but Edwin could not overcome his tremendous sense of loss. "I am as calm outwardly as though a wedding had taken place instead of a death," he wrote Richard Stoddard, who had returned to New York. "But, oh, the hell within me is intense! . . . My grief *eats* me!"

Dr. Samuel Osgood, the clergyman who had married Edwin and Mary, wrote to say he hoped Booth's art, his acting, would help to console him at this difficult time. The clergyman could not have been further off the mark. "I wish to God I was not an actor," Booth replied. "I despise and dread the d——d occupation; all its charms are gone and the stupid reality stands naked before me. I am a performing monkey, nothing more."

Edwin often talked of wanting to join Mary in death, and his friends feared he might take his own life. But then he slowly rallied. He had stopped shaving regularly and allowed his hair to grow long. Now he went to a barber for a haircut, and shaved off his stubbly beard. He still smoked twelve to fifteen cigars a day, and sometimes a pipe, and drank far too many cups of black coffee. But he vowed to give up the drinking, which he blamed for Mary's death. "I'll struggle—I'll fight—I'll conquer, too, with God's help," he wrote Richard Stoddard. After all, he had his daughter, Edwina—his and Mary's daughter—to look after and provide for.

He gave up the Dorchester house with its painful memories of his late wife, and moved with Edwina into a rented brownstone on East Seventeenth Street in New York City. His mother and sister Rosalie joined him there to help with Edwina's care. From that time on, he wrote to Adam Badeau, he was determined to be a more responsible person. "Mary's goodness was while here thrown away upon me," he wrote. "But it was not wasted, for now I feel it, now it shows as it ever will, my guiding star through life."

To prove to himself that he had really changed, he kept his vow to stay away from alcohol. But even though many of his friends urged it, he was reluctant to go back on the stage. It was while performing in New York before that he had lost control of himself and failed Mary. Now he feared he might do so again, but this time he would be failing his little daughter. "All my hopes and aspirations now are clustering like a halo about her head," he wrote to Badeau. "She is the light of my darkened life."

While Edwin was slowly putting his life back together, John was busy acting in one city after another. In April 1863, he began a season in Washington, D.C., playing the title role in *Richard III*. The posters for the occasion gave him top billing, proclaiming him "THE PRIDE OF THE AMERICAN PEOPLE, THE YOUNGEST TRAGEDIAN IN THE WORLD . . . A STAR OF THE FIRST MAGNITUDE, SON OF THE GREAT JUNIUS BRUTUS BOOTH, AND BROTHER AND ARTISTIC RIVAL OF EDWIN BOOTH."

The Washington critics were almost as enthusiastic as the theatre's copywriters. The *National Republican* called John's performance "a complete triumph" and said he "took the hearts of the audience by storm." The *National Intelligencer* said he possessed "that which is the grand constituent of all truly great acting, intensity. We have only to say that this young actor plays not from stage rule, but from his soul, and his soul is inspired with genius."

Washington in the second year of the Civil War bustled with activity. The streets were crowded with Union officers in their blue-and-gold uniforms, government employees hurrying to and from work, army wagons carrying supplies to the front, and other wagons bringing the wounded back from the battlefield for treatment in makeshift hospitals. People were hungry for entertainment of all sorts—anything that would distract them from

Although his brother Edwin was best known for his interpretation of Hamlet, John Wilkes Booth also played the role. Here is an unknown artist's portrayal of John in the part.
Evert Jansen Wendell Collection, The Harvard Theatre Collection, Houghton Library

the war—and the theater where John was starring was sold out for the entire week.

One of Washington's most ardent theatergoers was President Abraham Lincoln. He loved all kinds of shows, from slapstick farces to the loftiest Shakespearean tragedies, and he saw both Edwin and John Wilkes Booth act on several occasions. According to an anecdote, the president attended one of John's performances during the actor's spring 1863 season. Twice, when he made threats at another character in the play, John seemed to point toward Lincoln, who was sitting in the presidential box to the right of the stage. When Booth did it a third time, one of Lincoln's guests turned to the president and said, "Mr. Lincoln, he looks as if he meant that for you."

Playbill for John Wilkes Booth's appearance in *Hamlet*, part of his acclaimed spring 1863 season in Washington, D.C.
The Harvard Theatre Collection, Houghton Library

"Well," Lincoln is reported to have said of Booth, "he did look pretty sharp at me, didn't he?"

That story, recounted in Katherine Helm's book *The True Story of Mary, Wife of Lincoln,* may or may not be true. It's certainly a fact, however, that John Wilkes Booth loathed the president and everything he represented. And the actor continued to get into trouble for expressing his views in public. In St. Louis, Missouri, where he played after finishing his Washington engagement, John and another actor, T. L. Conner, were arrested for making "treasonous" remarks against the Lincoln administration.

Tensions ran high in Missouri, a border state in which Union loyalists often clashed with supporters of the Confederacy. In this heated atmosphere, Conner was given a sixty-day sentence in a military prison for his remarks, and John was brought before a military judge for having said he "wished the President and the whole damned government would go to hell." Not wanting his tour to be interrupted, John took an oath of allegiance to the Union and paid a stiff fine. This won him his release, but it did not change his views. If anything, the experience strengthened his conviction that he was in the right.

John's firmly held beliefs led to conflicts with members of his own family. In 1863, he was traveling by train from Philadelphia to New York with Asia's husband, John Sleeper Clarke. When Clarke made the mistake of speaking in a scornful way about the president of the Confederacy, Jefferson Davis, John took hold of the man and swung him around. Grabbing Clarke by the throat, John said, "Never, if you value your life, never speak in that way again of a man and a cause I hold sacred!" A shaken Clarke vowed that he wouldn't, and John relaxed his grip. Later, Clarke dismissed John's action as a "harmless temporary aberration," but relations between the two men were never the same again.

When John was in New York, he often stayed at Edwin's house so he could visit with their mother, who was living there. The two brothers continued to avoid discussing the war, knowing it would inevitably lead to friction between them. But still John felt the strain when they were together. "If it were not for mother I would not enter Edwin's house," he told Asia. "But she will leave there if I cannot be welcomed, and I do not want her to be unhappy because of me."

In July 1863, John finished his last engagement of the season at the Academy of Music in Cleveland and traveled by train to New York for a visit with his mother. He arrived at Edwin's house just as the bloodiest battle in the Civil War was reaching its gory conclusion. The Confederate commander, General Robert E. Lee, had led his forces in another invasion of the North and had gotten as far as Gettysburg, Pennsylvania, before he was stopped by a Union army under the command of General George G. Meade. By the time the fighting ended with Lee's withdrawal on July 4, more than 23,000 Union soldiers and 25,000 Confederate troops had died. Although it was not immediately evident, Gettysburg would mark a major turning point in the war, and the beginning of the Confederacy's decline as a fighting force.

Whatever John thought about the Battle of Gettysburg, he kept it to himself. But he let Asia know how strongly he felt about another violent event that occurred in July 1863, probably because he himself was on hand for it. With the war dragging on and no end in sight, Congress had passed a new Union Conscription Act. It made all able-bodied men from twenty to forty-five eligible for drafting into the Union army, but it allowed the well-to-do to escape service by providing a substitute or paying a $300 fee.

Resentment of the Conscription Act grew, especially among working-

General Robert E. Lee, commander of the Confederate Army.
Photo by Mathew Brady.
The National Archives

class Irish immigrants in New York City. The Irish feared that they would be forced to fight for the freedom of the slaves, who would then come north and take their jobs. Egged on by rabble-rousers, the immigrants gathered in a mob that exploded into riot on July 13. For four days the mob rampaged through New York, burning federal property, attacking newspaper offices, looting stores, and breaking into private homes. The rioters killed policemen who tried to stop them, burned down an orphanage for black children, and beat or murdered any African Americans who had the misfortune to cross their path. These horrific events, which became known as the Draft Riots, remain the worst civil disturbance in American history.

John found himself indirectly involved in the Draft Riots when he aided in the rescue of Edwin's good friend Adam Badeau. Badeau had been wounded in fighting near New Orleans and was recuperating from his injuries at a relative's home in New York. The house was in a district hard hit by rioters, and his friends feared for Badeau's safety. John volunteered to travel in a carriage through the riot-torn streets of the city and bring the wounded Badeau back to Edwin's house. The rescue mission was a success, and John helped carry Badeau to a room on one of the upper floors. There Edwin and his mother looked after him until the rioting died down and Badeau could be taken to the country. Later, John made light of his role in a conversation with Asia. "Imagine me," he said, "helping that wounded Yankee soldier with my rebel sinews!"

John was closer to Asia than to any of his other siblings. Growing up on the family farm in Maryland, they had played together as children while their older brothers, Edwin and June, were performing in far-off California. John had shared his secrets with Asia when they were little, and he still did now that they were adults. He frequently visited her at her home in Philadelphia, trying to schedule his visits when her husband was away on business. "We are as the Antipodes [exact opposites]," John once told Asia, "and I would never darken Clarke's door, but for you."

John stopped off to see Asia shortly after the Draft Riots in New York, and he denounced the North's attempts to enlist immigrant Irishmen in the Union army. "It is the unwisest move this country has yet made," he exclaimed. "The suave pressing of hordes of ignorant foreigners, buying up citizens before they land, to swell their armies." He became even more passionate as he went on. "The time will come . . . when the braggart North will groan at not being able to swear they fought the South man to man. If the North conquers us it will be by numbers only, not by native grit, not pluck, and not by devotion!"

"*If the North conquers us*—we are of the North," Asia said.

"Not I! Not I!" John said excitedly, according to his sister. "So help me holy God! My soul, life, and possessions are for the South."

"Why not go fight for her then?" Asia asked.

John sat silent in the darkening room, his thin face hard set, she reported. Then he said, "I have only an arm to give; my brains are worth twenty men, my money worth a hundred. I have free pass everywhere. My profession, my name, is my passport. My beloved precious money—oh, never beloved till now!—is the means, one of the means, by which I serve the South."

As he sat "smiling grimly," in Asia's words, she remembered a man, a stranger, who had come to her house a few days before and asked for "Doctor Booth." Now she wondered if the man had been looking for John.

"All right," her brother admitted. "I am he, if to be a doctor means a dealer in quinine."

"The drug that the North says is more in demand than food for the Southerners?" Asia asked.

"Yes," John said without hesitation.

Quinine was a drug obtained from the bark of a South American tree, and was used primarily in the treatment of malaria. At the time of the Civil War, before the discovery of painkillers and antibiotics, quinine was also one of the only remedies available for reducing pain and fever. Consequently, it was in great demand by army doctors on both sides of the conflict, and extremely expensive. According to Asia, John rejoiced that he

Asia Booth Clarke.
Courtesy the Putnam Publishing Group

not only had plenty of money to buy the drug but knew people who could supply him with the genuine article.

"How do you get it into the South?" Asia asked.

"Horse collars and so forth," he said with a laugh.

"You run the blockade?" The North had established an embargo—a blockade—on many goods that once were traded freely between North and South. Quinine was one of them.

"Yes," John said.

Asia knew now, she wrote, that her brother—her hero—was a spy and a blockade runner. "I set the terrible words before my eyes," she said, "and knew that each one meant death" if he were caught. She also realized that nothing she might say or do would persuade John to turn away from the path he had chosen. "He was today what he had been from childhood, an ardent lover of the South and her policy, an upholder of her principles," she wrote.

Chapter 10
"When Lincoln Shall Be King"

After much hesitation, and several postponements, Edwin finally returned to the stage on September 21, 1863, at the Winter Garden in New York. For his first appearance since his wife's death, he chose to play a character who also had trouble deciding what to do—Shakespeare's Hamlet. The reaction of the critics was mixed; some felt it was the best Hamlet they had ever seen, others found Edwin guilty of overacting. But the sold-out audience greeted his performance with warm-hearted applause.

For Edwin, the evening marked a triumph over his major weakness. His friends might worry that he was smoking too much, and downing too many cups of black coffee, but he was not drinking—that was the important thing. And when someone commented jokingly on his newfound abstinence, he responded with a fierce "I dare not, I dare not, I dare not!"

While Edwin was making his reluctant comeback that fall, John raced from one theatrical engagement to another. Between the end of September and the end of November, he played for two weeks in Boston, followed by brief stays in Providence, Rhode Island; Hartford, Connecticut; Brooklyn, New York; and then back to New Haven, Connecticut. John demanded and got high fees for his work: a nightly guarantee of $140, after which he would receive a share of the proceeds, and a benefit each week from which he would get all the proceeds. It's safe to assume that at least some of this money went to pay for the quinine and other scarce items that Booth was smuggling into the South.

At the beginning of November, John became one of the first leading actors to perform at the brand-new Ford's Theatre in Washington, D.C. Described by its owner as a "magnificent Thespian temple" (Thespis was a poet in ancient Greece, and often called the father of Greek tragedy), Ford's Theatre had excellent acoustics and seats for 2,400 spectators. On November 9, President Lincoln and his party were among those who crowded into Ford's to see John play a romantic young sculptor in the popular play *The Marble Heart*. Afterward, the president sent word backstage that he would like to meet the actor, but John, given his strong feelings about Lincoln, declined the invitation.

After his Washington engagement ended, John finished off the fall season with a four-day stay in Cleveland, Ohio. As in the other cities where he had played, he drew large crowds and was well paid for his efforts—almost $1,000 for the four performances. But perhaps because he had been working steadily without a break, he had grown tired of performing night after night. What were actors, anyway? he asked a colleague, and then went on to answer his own question: "Mummers of the quality of skimmed milk. They know little, think less, and understand next to nothing."

Eager to make even more money, John asked his representatives to bid on empty lots in the Back Bay section of Boston. He also invested in the booming oil business that had sprung up following the discovery of petroleum in western Pennsylvania. Meanwhile, he planned to get an early start on his spring season by giving nine performances in Leavenworth, Kansas, at the end of 1863. From there he would go on to St. Louis, Missouri, where he was scheduled to begin a two-week engagement on January 4, 1864. He allowed for four days' travel time between Leavenworth and St. Louis, which should have been more than enough. But he failed to take into account the unpredictable nature of winter weather in the Midwest.

John got as far as St. Joseph, Missouri, by riverboat before a fierce blizzard blew in across the plains. He had expected to travel on to St. Louis by train, but the storm halted all train travel in and out of St. Joseph. The temperature fell to twenty below zero, and some trains were reported to be buried west of the city in snowdrifts thirty feet deep. John wasn't prepared for the delay. Later, he wrote to a friend, "I have had a rough time since I last saw you. . . . In St. Joe I was down to my last cent, and had to give a dramatic reading to pay my way. It brought me $150." But he was still stuck in St. Joseph, with no prospect of relief from the snow and cold.

By now it was January 9, and he had already missed five of his scheduled performances in St. Louis. Determined to get there somehow, he hired a

Engraving of John Wilkes Booth in a fur-collared overcoat.
The Library of Congress

four-horse sleigh to travel sixty miles cross-country to Breckinridge, Missouri. He had heard that a few trains were running from there to St. Louis. Arriving half frozen in Breckinridge, he finally boarded a St. Louis–bound train, only to have it stall in a snowdrift less than an hour later. He told a friend he had to hold a pistol to the conductor's head to get the train moving again.

John opened in St. Louis at last on the evening of January 12, delighting the crowd with a rousing performance of *Richard III*. But some noted that his voice was hoarse, and not as strong as they remembered it from earlier appearances. Booth blamed the problem on the bitter cold he had endured riding across Missouri in an open sleigh. He finished the St. Louis engagement on a high note and traveled on without a pause to Louisville, Kentucky; Nashville, Tennessee; and Cincinnati, Ohio. Then he wrapped up his swing through the Midwest and South with a three-week stay in New Orleans, Louisiana. John's vocal problems continued to dog him, however, and theater critics began to comment on them. The reviewer for the *New Orleans Picayune* wrote, "His first performance . . . disappointed us. His elocution appeared to be deficient in clearness and very labored."

The condition didn't improve as the New Orleans run progressed. In a later review, the *New Orleans Times* critic wrote that John had given a vivid impersonation of Richard III, but "his raucous voice kept him from being up to his usual standard." The next night, the critic was pleased with John's overall performance as Othello while expressing regret that "a severe hoarseness marred his articulation." His voice was no better the next night, when he played the title role in Shakespeare's *Macbeth,* and by the following day it had given out entirely. That evening's edition of the *Times* carried the following notice:

> The management of the St. Charles Theatre regrets to inform the public that in consequence of the severe and continued cold under which Mr. Booth has been laboring for several days, and at the suggestion of his medical adviser, he is compelled to take a short respite from his engagement. Due notice will be given of his next appearance.

The notice didn't tell the entire truth. John and his doctors sensed that his hoarseness wasn't the product of a severe cold but resulted from the constant misuse of his voice. Only a long rest and regular vocal exercises might correct the problem, but John couldn't afford to take the time for that. He had more pressing concerns on his mind—namely, the hard-pressed Southern cause. And so, after just one day off, and with his voice still raspy, he returned to the theater and a week later concluded his engagement in New Orleans.

While John was on the road that winter and spring, Edwin stayed closer to home. He bought a brownstone house on East Nineteenth Street in New

York and limited his appearances to New York and other Eastern cities so that he could spend more time with his daughter, Edwina. She was two now, old enough to enjoy the poems her father read to her in the evening before she went to bed and he left for the theater. He would cradle her in his lap, his left arm clasped around her, while he recited verses by Alfred, Lord Tennyson, and other poets:

> *What does little birdie say*
> *In her nest at peep of day?*

Back home at midnight, he would stop by the door to Edwina's room or stand by her crib and watch his darling sleep. "Good night, my little birdie," he would whisper before going to bed himself.

Following in his brother John's footsteps, Edwin starred in a series of plays at the new Ford's Theatre in Washington. Secretary of State William H. Seward gave a dinner in Edwin's honor, and President and Mrs. Lincoln came to see him in Shakespeare's *The Merchant of Venice*. Afterward the president was quoted as saying: "A good performance, but I'd a thousand times rather read it at home if it were not for Booth's playing."

On a visit to Philadelphia, Edwin finally mended the rift that had developed between him and his sister Asia as a result of her dislike of his late wife. He also entered into a business arrangement with her husband, John Sleeper Clarke, with whom John Wilkes had often clashed. Clarke and Edwin signed contracts to take over the leases of the Walnut Street Theatre in Philadelphia and the Winter Garden in New York. Now Edwin would be a theater manager as well as an actor, and if all went well, he would have an income from the rental of his theaters even when he wasn't performing on their stages.

John Wilkes took a three-week break to rest and restore his health after finishing his troubled run in New Orleans. However, his voice was still somewhat hoarse when he embarked on one of the most demanding engagements of his theatrical career. On April 25, 1864, he opened a four-week run in Boston, during which he gave thirty-four performances in eighteen different plays, in all of which he played the leading role!

A few of the Boston drama critics commented on John's vocal problems, but their reviews were generally favorable. And audiences responded more enthusiastically to John than ever before. As one journalist wrote, "Crowded houses have thus far attended the performances of J. Wilkes Booth. . . . Seats are in demand for a week ahead, and there is every indication that his present visit to Boston will be crowned with greater success than any heretofore made." Neither John nor his fans had any way of knowing it then, but the actor's month-long stay in Boston would be the last major theatrical engagement of his career.

While John and Edwin were performing in various cities in the spring of 1864, the opposing armies in the Civil War had become locked in a stalemate. The Union general Ulysses S. Grant confronted the Confederate leader, Robert E. Lee, in the trenches outside Petersburg, Virginia, and another Union general, William Tecumseh Sherman, had entered northern Georgia. There had been tremendous losses on both sides. In just four months, the Union and Confederate armies had each lost more than 90,000 of their best fighting men.

In the meantime, a presidential election campaign was looming. The Republican Party held its convention in Baltimore in June and, as expected, nominated Abraham Lincoln for a second term. His reelection was far from a sure thing, however. The ever-increasing numbers of dead and wounded led many, including some Republicans, to dub Lincoln "Abe the Widowmaker." Their doubts about him were only reinforced when he issued a call in mid-July for 500,000 more soldiers. Would the fighting just go on and on, without any foreseeable end?

The Democratic Party reflected even greater dissatisfaction with Lincoln's leadership. Calling his military policies a failure, the Democrats nominated General George C. McClellan for president. McClellan, in accepting the nomination, said that he believed in carrying on the war until it was won, but he did not rule out compromise and reconciliation.

Many Northerners welcomed General McClellan's moderate tone in that war-weary summer of 1864. Even some of Lincoln's staunchest Republican supporters came to think that the President stood little chance of reelection. A prominent New York politician put it bluntly: "Nobody here doubts it [that Lincoln will be defeated]; nor do I see anybody from other states who authorizes the slightest hope of success. . . . The people are wild for peace."

These developments must have been reassuring to John Wilkes Booth and given him hope that the South might still be victorious in the war. However, he made no mention of politics in the letters that he wrote at the time. John had a gift for keeping his various relationships and activities in separate compartments. For example, in the summer of 1864, he carried on a passionate correspondence with Isabel Sumner, the sixteen-year-old daughter of a Boston merchant, whom he had met while performing in Boston that spring.

"How shall I write you; as *lover, friend,* or *brother*?" John asked Isabel in his first letter to her. "I think *so much* of you, that (at your bidding) I would even try to school my heart to beat as the latter. The first and second would require no exertion, for the *first* (forgive me) I cannot help being, and the second, *I am,* and hope I ever shall be."

While he was corresponding with Isabel that summer, John made a three-week trip to western Pennsylvania to inspect the oil fields he'd invested in. Then, in late July, he paid a brief visit to Boston. He probably saw Isabel during his stay in her home city, but the main purpose of the trip was apparently to meet with several Confederate spies at the Parker House Hotel.

The latest news from the Civil War battlefronts was not encouraging for those who supported the South. General Lee had held the line in Virginia, but the Union army under General Sherman was advancing steadily toward Atlanta, Georgia. It's not known if John discussed these events with the Southern agents at the Parker House. But in the weeks following their meeting, John embarked on a bold new scheme to aid the South—a scheme that involved far greater risks than the smuggling of quinine.

In 1862, the Union and the Confederacy had reached an agreement to conduct regular exchanges of prisoners of war. The agreement hit a snag, though, when the North began to enlist black troops in the Union army. The South threatened to treat captured African-American soldiers as runaway slaves, and the North retaliated by halting all prisoner exchanges in April 1864. At that time, more than 200,000 Confederate prisoners were being held in Northern prisons.

The suspension of the exchanges hit the South far harder than the North because the Confederate army had always been outnumbered by the Union forces. Neither side was willing to compromise on the issue of the black troops, however, and by the summer of 1864, the South faced a crucial lack of manpower. It was at this point that either John or the Confederate agents he met with in Boston came up with a far-fetched plan to solve the problem. John would organize a group of Confederate sympathizers, and together they would kidnap President Lincoln and hold him for ransom until all Confederate prisoners of war were released.

Whoever thought of the plan, John immediately began to lay the groundwork for carrying it out. Adding urgency to the scheme was the fall of Atlanta to General Sherman's troops on September 2. This defeat would prove to be another major turning point in the war. Not only did the South lose a major railroad center and more than 20,000 of its best soldiers, but the Union victory also gave President Lincoln's reelection chances a tremendous boost.

Later in September, soon after Northern newspapers hailed the fall of

John Wilkes Booth in a contemplative mood.
Shaw Collection, The Harvard Theatre Collection, Houghton Library

Atlanta, John traveled to Baltimore. There he invited two boyhood friends, Samuel Arnold and Michael O'Laughlin, to visit him in his hotel room. Arnold had recently been discharged from the Confederate army, and O'Laughlin had also fought for the South. The two men remained sympathetic to the Confederate cause, and they listened intently as John, over wine and cigars, laid out the details of the plot.

President Lincoln had a getaway cottage on the grounds of the Soldiers' Home in the hills outside Washington, John explained. The president frequently traveled to the cottage in an unguarded carriage. It would be easy, John said, to force the carriage to a halt, subdue the driver, and take the president captive. Then they would drive the carriage across the Anacostia River bridge into southern Maryland. If the sentries on the bridge tried to stop them, they would gun them down.

Once they were safely in Maryland, they would race across the state to Port Tobacco on the Potomac River, where a small boat would be waiting for them. They would cross the wide river to Virginia under cover of darkness and hurry on to Richmond, the Confederate capital. If all went well, Abraham Lincoln would be a prisoner of the Confederacy less than a day after his capture in Washington.

John made a persuasive case for the plan, and when he had finished, both Arnold and O'Laughlin agreed to sign on to it. The three men parted, with John promising to be in touch again as soon as he had more definite information. Meanwhile, sometime in August he had broken off his relationship with Isabel Sumner. With the kidnapping plot in the works, Booth had little time to think of romance. He also brushed aside all offers of acting engagements for the fall-and-winter season.

In October, John told friends he was going to Buffalo to fulfill a theater commitment. Instead, he traveled to Montreal and registered at a hotel that served as a sort of headquarters for Confederate agents stationed in Canada. No records exist of what transpired during Booth's ten-day stay in Montreal, but it's assumed that he received approval for the kidnapping plot and funds to help execute it. He had brought with him to Canada his trunk of theatrical costumes and props—worth an estimated $25,000— and he made arrangements to have the trunk shipped by boat to a destination in Virginia. Apparently, he intended to resume his acting career in the South once he'd carried out the kidnapping of the president.

Booth returned to the United States in late October and bought two rifles, several revolvers, three daggers, and two pairs of handcuffs from an arms dealer in New York. Not wanting to risk having the weapons found in his luggage, he had them shipped to Samuel Arnold in Baltimore. He himself traveled to southern Maryland to scout the escape route they would take once Lincoln had been captured. There he was introduced to a strong supporter of the Confederacy, Dr. Samuel Mudd. Mudd was not unique; although Maryland was part of the Union, the southern section of the state was filled with Confederate sympathizers.

From Maryland, Booth journeyed north to Philadelphia for another visit with Asia. It was now early November, shortly before Election Day. Judging by Asia's account of the visit, John told her he'd just been in southern Maryland but said nothing about the kidnapping plot. He was obviously upset about the course of the war. One night, according to Asia, her brother was "more than usually excited; he looked haggard and worn. I heard him murmur, 'Oh, God, grant me to see the end!'"

Asia urged him not to go south again, but he replied, "Well, where should I go then?" He followed the question by singing, in a low voice, a satiric song that ended, "In 1865, when Lincoln shall be king . . ."

"Oh, not that," Asia said. "That will *never* come to pass."

"No, by God's mercy," John said, jumping to his feet. "Never that!" Then, according to Asia, he whispered fiercely that Lincoln should never have been president. "This man's appearance, his pedigree, his coarse low jokes and anecdotes, his vulgar similes, and his policy are a disgrace to the seat he holds. Other brains rule the country. *He* is made the tool of the North to crush out, or try to crush out, slavery by robbery, rape, slaughter, and bought armies."

John's voice, Asia said, rose as he continued: "*He* is Bonaparte [Napoleon Bonaparte, former Emperor of France] in one great move, that is, by overturning this blind Republic and making himself a king. This man's reelection, I tell you, will be a reign! . . . You'll see, you'll see, that *reelection* means *succession*. His kin and friends are in every place of office already. . . . [Lincoln is] a false president yearning for kingly succession as hotly as ever did Ariston [an ancient Greek tyrant]."

Asia didn't know what to say in response. She could only listen patiently, she wrote, to "these wild tirades, which were the very fever of his

[John's] distracted brain and tortured heart." His passionate beliefs ran so deep that she felt herself "powerless to check or soothe" them.

On November 8, as John had predicted, Abraham Lincoln was elected to a second term as president, easily defeating his Democratic opponent. John's reaction to Lincoln's victory was not immediately apparent. By then he was in New York, rehearsing for what would be his only stage appearance that fall, and the only time he would act in a play with both of his older brothers, June and Edwin. June had come east that summer for his first visit in many years. Edwin, remembering all the favors his older brother had done him in California, hired June to help run the Winter Garden.

June's return gave Edwin another idea. New York's Central Park was then under construction, and park officials had sought a contribution from Edwin for the statue of William Shakespeare that was planned for the Mall. Instead of giving a cash donation, Edwin proposed that he stage a benefit performance, all proceeds from which would go toward the cost of the statue. The park officials were delighted with the idea, and even more pleased when Edwin said he intended to make the benefit a real event. He would costar for the first time on any stage with his brothers June and John Wilkes in a production of Shakespeare's *Julius Caesar*. Edwin would play the conflicted Brutus, June would portray Cassius of the "lean and hungry look," and John would impersonate the handsome and dashing Marc Anthony.

June and John both responded enthusiastically to Edwin's plan, and John went so far as to shave off his trademark mustache for the role of Anthony. But even as John plunged into rehearsals for the play, he was thinking ahead to his next venture. He planned to move his base of operations to Washington and enlist more recruits in the kidnapping plot. Then he would decide on the best time and place to seize the president—the man, John was convinced, who aimed to make himself king of the United States.

Chapter 11
"To Whom It May Concern"

*A*s soon as posters went up announcing the joint appearance of "the three sons of the great Booth" in *Julius Caesar*, there was a rush to the box office at the Winter Garden. Seat prices for regular performances ranged from fifteen to seventy-five cents, but for this special benefit, balcony seats cost $1.00, while the best seats in the orchestra went for a whopping $5.00. These prices didn't faze ardent theater lovers, however. They were so eager to see the three Booths onstage together that all 2,000 seats were snapped up quickly, raising more than $4,000 toward the cost of the Shakespeare statue.

On the night of the performance, Mary Ann Booth sat in a private box to the right of the stage. When the curtain fell at the end of Act I, she looked down proudly as her three sons came out from behind the curtain. They acknowledged the audience's shouts of "Bravo!" and then turned to bow in unison to their mother. Asia, watching from an orchestra seat, gave a vivid description of the scene: "The theatre was crowded to suffocation, people sitting and standing in every available place. . . . The three brothers received and merited the applause of the immense audience, for they acted well and presented a picture too strikingly heroic to be soon forgotten."

The reviewer for the *New York Herald* was equally enthusiastic. He reported that "the vast audience was fairly carried by storm from the first entrance of the three brothers side by side. . . . [Edwin Booth's] Brutus was individualized with great force and distinctness—[Junius Booth's] Cassius was brought out equally well—and if there was less of real personality given Marc Antony, the fault was rather in the part than in the actor. . . . He [John Wilkes Booth] played with a phosphorescent passion and fire, which recalled to old theatregoers the characteristics of [his father] the elder Booth." None of the reviewers said anything about John having vocal problems; apparently the months he had spent away from the stage had given his voice time to heal.

The only thing that marred the gala evening was an incident at the beginning of the second act. Shortly after the curtain rose, firemen rushed into the lobby of the Winter Garden shouting "Fire! Fire!" Audience members exchanged anxious glances, and some rose in their seats and started to push toward the exits. Panic threatened until Edwin walked down to the footlights and reassured the crowd that there was nothing to fear. The blaze was next door in the Lafarge House hotel, he said, and the city's firemen had already brought it under control. His words had the desired effect. Those who had begun to leave the theater returned to their seats, and the performance continued without any further interruptions.

The next morning, over breakfast at Edwin's home, the brothers read in the newspaper that the Lafarge House

Playbill for the benefit performance of Shakespeare's *Julius Caesar* starring the three Booth brothers.
The Harvard Theatre Collection, Houghton Library

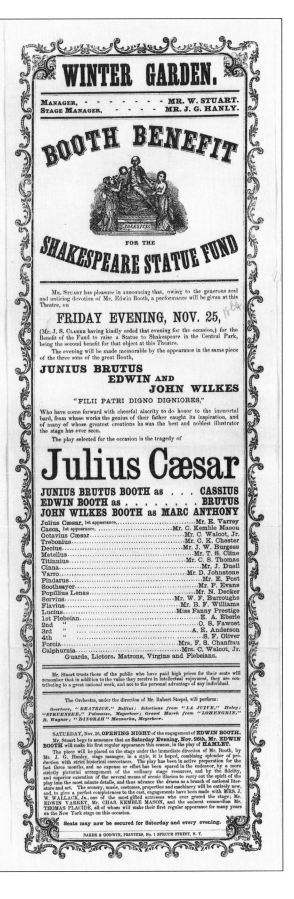

WINTER GARDEN.

MANAGER, - - - - - - MR. W. STUART.
STAGE MANAGER, - - - - - MR. J. G. HANLY.

BOOTH BENEFIT

FOR THE

SHAKESPEARE STATUE FUND

Mr. Stuart has pleasure in announcing that, owing to the generous zeal and untiring devotion of Mr. Edwin Booth, a performance will be given at this Theatre, on

FRIDAY EVENING, NOV. 25,

(Mr. J. S. Clarke having kindly ceded that evening for the occasion,) for the Benefit of the Fund to raise a Statue to Shakespeare in the Central Park, being the second benefit for that object at this Theatre.

The evening will be made memorable by the appearance in the same piece of the three sons of the great Booth,

JUNIUS BRUTUS
EDWIN AND
JOHN WILKES

"FILII PATRI DIGNO DIGNIORES,"

Who have come forward with cheerful alacrity to do honor to the immortal bard, from whose works the genius of their father caught its inspiration, and of many of whose greatest creations he was the best and noblest illustrator the stage has ever seen.

The play selected for the occasion is the tragedy of

Julius Cæsar

JUNIUS BRUTUS BOOTH as . . . . CASSIUS
EDWIN BOOTH as . . . . BRUTUS
JOHN WILKES BOOTH as MARC ANTHONY

Julius Cæsar, 1st appearance, ...Mr. E. Varrey
Casca, 1st appearance, ...Mr. C. Kemble Mason
Octavius Cæsar.....................................Mr. C. Walcot, Jr.
Trebonius..Mr. C. K. Chester
Decius..Mr. J. W. Burgess
Metellus...Mr. T. S. Cline
Titinnius..Mr. C. S. Thomas
Cinna...Mr. J. Duell
Varro...Mr. D. Johnstone
Pindarus..Mr. E. Post
Soothsayer...Mr. P. Evans
Popillius Lenas......................................Mr. N. Decker
Servius..Mr. W. F. Burroughs
Flavius...Mr. B. F. Williams
Lucius...Miss Fanny Prestige
1st Plebeian..E. A. Eberle
2nd   "   ....O. S. Fawcet
3rd   "   ....A. E. Anderson
4th   "   ....S. F. Oliver
Porcia..Mrs. F. S. Chanfrau
Calphurnia..Mrs. C. Walcot, Jr.
Guards, Lictors, Matrons, Virgins and Plebeians.

Mr. Stuart trusts those of the public who have paid high prices for their seats will remember that in addition to the value they receive in intellectual enjoyment, they are contributing to a great national work, and not to the personal advantage of any individual.

The Orchestra, under the direction of Mr. Robert Stoepel, will perform:

Overture, "BEATRICE," Bellini; Selections from "LA JUIVE," Halcy; "STRUENSEE," Polonaise, Meyerbeer; Grand March from "LOHENGRIN," R. Wagner; "DINORAH" Mazourka, Meyerbeer.

SATURDAY, Nov. 26, OPENING NIGHT of the engagement of EDWIN BOOTH.
Mr. Stuart begs to announce that on Saturday Evening, Nov. 26th, Mr. EDWIN BOOTH will make his first regular appearance this season, in the play of HAMLET.
The piece will be placed on the stage under the immediate direction of Mr. Booth, by Mr. J. G. Hanley, stage manager, in a style, it is hoped, combining splendor of production with strict historical correctness. The play has been in active preparation for the last three months, and no expense or effort has been spared in the endeavor, by a more strictly pictorial arrangement of the ordinary stage resources, and by the fidelity and superior execution of the several means of scenic illusion to carry out the spirit of the play into the most minute details, and thus advance the drama as a branch of national literature and art. The scenery, music, costumes, properties and machinery will be entirely new, and, to give a perfect completeness to the cast, engagements have been made with MRS. J. W. WALLACK, Jr., one of the most gifted actresses who ever graced the stage; Mr. EDWIN VARREY, Mr. CHAS. KEMBLE MASON, and the unrivaled comedian Mr. THOMAS PLACIDE, all of whom will make their first regular appearance for many years on the New York stage on this occasion.

Seats may now be secured for Saturday and every evening.

BAKER & GODWIN, PRINTERS, No. 1 SPRUCE STREET, N. Y.

Scene from the benefit performance of *Julius Caesar* with, left to right, John Wilkes Booth as Marc Anthony, Edwin Booth as Brutus, and Junius Booth Jr. as Cassius.

The Harvard Theatre Collection, Houghton Library

fire was just one of a dozen that had been set the night before in hotels and public buildings throughout New York. The police believed the fires were the work of Confederate agents who wanted to demoralize the city's residents and turn them against the government's Civil War policies. A widespread hunt was on for those responsible, the report said, and police officials expected to announce arrests shortly.

The fires, and the speculation about who had set them, brought to the surface the Booth brothers' sharply differing political views. June, who was accustomed to the rough justice of the West, said that in San Francisco such arsonists would be rounded up by the city's vigilance committee and hanged in a public square. Edwin blamed the violence on the war and disclosed that, several weeks earlier, he had voted for Lincoln's reelection, hoping the president would be able to achieve peace at last.

At this, John exploded in anger. He claimed that the fires in New York were retaliation for the destruction the Union army had wrought on its march through Georgia. And he told Edwin he'd regret his vote for Lincoln when the president made the United States a monarchy and had himself crowned king. The breakfast-table conversation became so heated that Edwin finally issued an ultimatum to his brother. According to an account by Adam Badeau, "John Wilkes declared his wish for the success of the Rebellion [the Confederacy] so decidedly that Edwin finally told him he should go elsewhere to make such sentiments known; that he was not at liberty to express them in the house of a Union supporter."

There is no record of what Mary Ann Booth thought of this rupture between her sons. But John's banishment from Edwin's house must have upset her greatly, for she looked forward to her younger son's frequent visits. As for Edwin and John, they had other things on their minds. In his dual role as comanager and actor, Edwin was heavily involved in a new production of *Hamlet* that was scheduled to open at the Winter Garden the night after the *Julius Caesar* benefit. Edwin and his partners had spared no expense on the sets and costumes for *Hamlet*, and Edwin, as he prepared to play the title role, delved more deeply into the character than he ever had before.

All of Edwin's efforts paid off handsomely. Audiences thrilled to the spectacular scenery and lavish costumes, and listened in rapt silence as Booth delivered Hamlet's famous soliloquies: "Oh, God! Oh, God! How weary, stale, flat, and unprofitable Seem to me all the uses of this world . . ." and "To be, or not to be, That is the question. . . ." The critics had nothing but praise for the production and Edwin's performance. William Winter wrote: "Edwin Booth's Hamlet is the simple, absolute realization of Shakespeare's haunted prince." The *New York Times* summed up his interpretation in a single sentence: "Hamlet is a part in which he [Booth] has no living equal." Edwin had guessed the production might run four weeks in New York; instead, it ran twelve, breaking all records for a Shakespearean play up to that time. His friends said they had not seen Booth look so happy since the days of his marriage.

Meanwhile, John Wilkes's activities pointed in a very different direction. Following the *Julius Caesar* benefit, he returned to Washington and rented rooms at the National Hotel. There he enlisted new members in the kidnapping plot: Lewis Powell, a stocky, fearless Confederate veteran who would bring muscle to the operation; Davey Herold, a young man familiar with the back roads of southern Maryland; and John Harrison Surratt, an experienced Confederate courier whose mother, Mary, ran a boarding house in Washington. Lastly, John recruited George Atzerodt, a boatman living in Port Tobacco, Maryland. Atzerodt would ferry the kidnap party— including a captive President Lincoln—across the Potomac River to Virginia.

Sometime in late 1864, John apparently felt a need to set down his thoughts and beliefs before taking action against the president. He expressed his feelings in two letters that were not intended to be delivered until later. In the first, addressed simply "To Whom It May Concern," he attempted to justify his support of the South and of slavery: "This country was formed for the *white* and not for the black man." He claimed that Southern blacks were better off under slavery: "I have lived among it most of my life and have seen *less* harsh treatment from Master to Slave than I have beheld in the north from father to son."

He went on to denounce the abolitionists as "the only traitors in the land," because, according to him, they had forced the South to secede in order to defend its rights. Thus the abolitionists were responsible, in his eyes, for the bloody Civil War that had brought so much suffering and death to both North and South. In conclusion, he tried to excuse what he was about to do, saying: "My love (as things stand today) is for the South alone. Nor do I deem it a dishonor in attempting to make for her a prisoner of this man [President Lincoln], to whom she owes so much of misery." He signed the letter: "A Confederate doing duty *upon his own responsibility.* J Wilkes Booth."

The second, and more personal, letter was addressed to his mother. "Dearest beloved Mother," it began. ". . . I have always endeavored to be a good and dutiful son. And even now would wish to die sooner than give you pain. But dearest Mother, though I owe you all, *there* is another duty. A noble duty for the sake of liberty and humanity due to my Country [by which he means the South]. For four years I have lived a *slave* in the north (a favored slave it's true, but no less hateful to me on that account). Not daring to express my thoughts or sentiments, even in my own home. Constantly hearing every principle, dear to my heart, denounced as treasonable."

He goes on to tell his mother that he has held his tongue mostly for her sake, knowing how hard it would be for her if he left the North. But now he feels he must go and "share the sufferings of my brave countrymen." He asks for her understanding and forgiveness, and expresses the hope that he will survive the war "by the grace of God." But "should the last bolt strike your son, dear Mother, bear it patiently. And think at the best life is but short, and *not at all times happy.* My Brothers and Sisters (Heaven protect them) will add my love and duty to their own, and watch you with care and kindness, till we meet again. And if *that happiness* does not come to us on earth, then may, O May it be with God."

He ended the letter by saying, "Come weal or woe, with never ending love and devotion, you will find me ever your affectionate son. John."

Once the two letters were finished, he sealed them and locked them in a drawer with his other important papers. Later he would give them to Asia for safekeeping.

January 1865 proved to be an unusually busy month for John—and not just in connection with the kidnapping plot. He continued to reject the many acting offers he received from cities around the country but agreed to take part in a benefit in Washington for an actress friend, Avonia Stanhope Jones. The two costarred in a production of Shakespeare's *Romeo and Juliet.* Given John's lack of interest in the theater at the moment, it was ironic that the Washington drama critics greeted his performance with

John Wilkes Booth in 1864.
*Shaw Collection, The Harvard Theatre
Collection, Houghton Library*

John Wilkes Booth,

some of the best reviews he'd ever received. The *National Intelligencer* raved, "No such Romeo has ever trod the boards. What perfect acting! His death scene was the most remarkable and fearfully natural that we have seen for years upon the stage."

John also found time for romance. He was often seen around Washington with an old girlfriend, Ella Starr, whose sister Nellie ran one of the city's most elegant and expensive brothels. But the main object of his affections was Lucy Hale, the beautiful younger daughter of John B. Hale, a former senator from New Hampshire. John Wilkes met Lucy sometime in January, when she and her family checked into the National Hotel, where he was staying. Lucy's father, an ardent abolitionist and strong supporter of

President Lincoln, had been defeated for reelection the previous fall. Now, as compensation, the president planned to name him ambassador to Spain, and Hale and his family had come to Washington for the announcement before going to Madrid.

It's not known whether the senator was aware of his daughter's growing involvement with John. If he was, it's doubtful that he approved of it, since actors generally were considered to be disreputable, and John was widely known as a ladies' man. But Booth made it clear to friends and family that he cared deeply about Lucy. His brother June said that John had told him "he was in love with a lady in Washington who was worth more to him than all the money he could make." For her part, Lucy made no bones about her feelings for John. She told close friends that she planned to return from Spain within a year, and when she did, she would marry John, with or without her father's blessing.

John's overriding concern, however, was the scheme to abduct the president. And as the weeks passed, and January shifted into February, the need to find an opportunity to carry out the plan became ever more urgent. From Atlanta, General Sherman's army had turned northward. Now his troops were advancing rapidly through South Carolina. If John and his cohorts were to secure the release of the Confederate prisoners, and thus turn the tide of the war in the South's favor, they would have to act—and act quickly.

Before he could do anything, though, John had to solve another problem; he was running out of ready cash. The cost of buying weapons and supplies, and paying the living expenses of the men he'd enlisted in the kidnapping plot, had depleted the funds he'd put aside from his last theatrical tour. In February, he made a trip to Philadelphia and New York, probably to borrow money from friends or arrange loans from other sources.

During the Philadelphia stopover, he paid a visit to Asia. She described the meeting in her memoirs. Sitting in her parlor on the last night of his stay, John said, "Let me show you the cipher." (The cipher was a secret code he had devised.)

Asia refused, saying she did not want to know about any cipher or code. But John pressed the point. "I might possibly need to communicate with you about my money affairs," he said, "and there is no need to let everyone know what I am worth."

She continued to resist the idea until he took a packet of papers from his breast pocket. Among the papers were the letters he had written several months before "To Whom It May Concern" and to his mother. "Lock this in your safe for me," John said, handing Asia the packet. "I may come back for it, but if anything should happen to me open the packet *alone* and send the letters as directed, and the money and papers give to their owners."

Asia did not consider her brother's request unusual. An actor's life involved constant travel, which was always rough and difficult then—especially in wartime. Accidents of one kind or another could so easily happen. She promised to lock up the packet, and John kissed her goodbye. But as she sat looking at the large envelope with the one word "Asia" written on it, he returned and said, "Let me *see* you lock it up."

Together they entered the room off the parlor that contained an iron safe. Asia stooped and placed the packet in it. Then she locked the safe and put the key in its hiding place. Before he left, John kissed her tenderly and said, "God bless you, sister mine. Take care of yourself, and try to be happy."

"Oh, my boy, I shall never be happy till I see your face again," she replied with all the anxiety of her heart, as she wrote later.

Back in Washington, John continued to meet with his fellow conspirators. They were growing impatient as the weeks went by and still no opportunity arose to put their kidnap scheme into action. Meanwhile, the Union was gradually closing in on the Confederacy. Charleston, South Carolina, where the war had begun at Fort Sumter, fell to Union forces on February 18. At the same time, Sherman's army seized the state capital, Columbia, and marched relentlessly on toward North Carolina. If John and his cohorts didn't do something soon, it would be too late to affect the outcome of the war.

President Lincoln's second inauguration was set for Saturday, March 4. John attended the event, thanks to a ticket Lucy Hale had obtained for him from her father. He passed easily through the police lines guarding the east front of the Capitol and stood in a spot not far from where Lincoln would take the oath of office and deliver his second inaugural address. It had rained all morning, but as Lincoln began to speak, the sun broke through the clouds. "With malice toward none, with charity for all; with firmness in the right, as God give us to see the right, let us strive on to finish the work we are in," Lincoln said.

President Abraham Lincoln speaks at his second inauguration, March 4, 1865. John Wilkes Booth was among those in the crowd watching the president.
The Library of Congress

John's reaction to the president's determined words is not known. But an indication of his feelings can be gathered from something he said afterward to an actor friend, Samuel Chester. "What an excellent chance I had to kill the President, if I had wished, on inauguration day!" Booth told him, according to testimony Chester gave later to police investigators.

While he waited for an opportunity to abduct Lincoln, John prepared himself for any eventuality. He purchased a derringer—a small, easy-to-conceal pistol that had a deadly effect at close range—and paid regular visits to a shooting gallery on Pennsylvania Avenue to practice his marksmanship. At the same time, his relationship with Lucy Hale was growing stronger by the day. The two exchanged poems declaring their love, and early in March they became secretly engaged.

John's mother was troubled about her son. According to Ann Hartley Gilbert, an actress who knew the family well, Mrs. Booth had a sort of sixth sense about John. "The love and sympathy between him and his mother were very close," Mrs. Gilbert wrote in her memoirs. "No matter how far apart they were, she seemed to know in some mysterious way when anything was wrong with him. . . . If he were ill, or unable to act, he would often receive a letter of sympathy, counsel and warning, written when she could not possibly have received any news of him."

That's what happened now. Mrs. Booth wrote John that she'd had "fearful" dreams about him, and she urged him to leave Washington and come to New York. She doubted if he would, however, for she'd heard of his involvement with Lucy Hale. "Edwin was told by someone that you were paying great attention to a fine young lady in Washington," Mrs. Booth wrote, and she went on to offer some maternal advice: "You have so often been in love and this may prove like the others, not of any lasting impression. . . . Think and reflect, and if the lady in question is all you desire, I see no cause why you should not try to secure her."

But Mrs. Booth was well aware of the general public's low opinion of actors. "Her father, I see, has his appointment [as ambassador to Spain]. Would he give his consent? You can but ask. . . . You know in my partial eyes you are a fit match for any woman, no matter who she may be—but some fathers have higher notions. God grant, if it is to be so, it will prove a source of happiness to you both."

As she drew the letter to a close, his mother could not resist injecting a wistful note: "Now I am going to dinner by myself. Why are you not here to chat and keep me company? No, you are saying soft things to one who doesn't love you half as well as your old mother does. God bless you, my dear darling boy. It's natural it should be so, I know, so I won't complain. I cannot expect to have you always. God guard you forever and ever. Your loving mother, Mary Ann."

John did not answer her letter right away. He had other, more pressing matters on his mind, including a bold new plan to kidnap the president.

Chapter 12
"SIC SEMPER TYRANNIS!"

On March 15, John invited his fellow conspirators to join him for a performance at Ford's Theatre. He had arranged for them to sit in the state box—the box President Lincoln occupied when he attended the theater. Afterward, the group gathered for a midnight supper at Gautier's, an expensive restaurant in downtown Washington. John had reserved a private room for the occasion so that no other diners could listen in as he outlined his scheme. As John laid it out, the new plan to kidnap the president sounded like a scene from one of the melodramas in which Booth had often acted. The next time Lincoln attended a performance at Ford's Theatre, John and Lewis Powell would enter the state box and seize him. At that moment, two of the other conspirators, Michael O'Laughlin and Davey Herold, would extinguish all the gaslights in the theater.

In the darkness and confusion that followed, Samuel Arnold would jump up onto the stage from a seat in the first row and help Booth and Powell lower the president down from the box. The conspirators would hurry Lincoln out a door at the back of the theater and force him into a horse-drawn carriage waiting in the alley. The group would make their getaway before anyone could stop them and drive swiftly to the eastern branch of the Potomac. There John Surratt and George Atzerodt would be waiting to convey Lincoln across the river to Maryland in a boat that John had purchased.

When he had finished describing the scheme, John asked for comments. Some of the conspirators thought the plan would work, others questioned one or another part of it. Samuel Arnold brought the discussion to an abrupt end when he said he had signed on for a military operation, not a suicide pact. "I wanted a shadow of a chance for success and escape,"

Arnold testified later, and he didn't think John's idea offered either. Others in the group agreed with Arnold, and the gathering finally broke up at five A.M. leaving an angry and disappointed John to ponder his next move.

A fresh opportunity came sooner than he might have expected. On the morning of March 17, John learned that President Lincoln planned to travel to the Seventh Street Hospital that afternoon to attend an entertainment for wounded soldiers. Booth quickly rallied his colleagues, and by three o'clock they were all on horseback and riding out on Seventh Street in the direction of the hospital. Their plan, according to testimony John Surratt gave later at his trial, was to pull alongside the president's carriage on its return to the city and force it to the side of the road. One of their party would then jump onto the driver's seat and take control of the horses. The others in the group would climb into the carriage and restrain the president. Then the driver would swing the carriage around and head directly for southern Maryland via Benning's Bridge.

This new scheme might have succeeded if all had gone according to plan —but it didn't. At the last minute, the president decided not to travel to the hospital after all, so John and his colleagues made their ride for nothing. John Surratt, in his testimony, called the failed expedition "a bitter disappointment." He added, "It was our last attempt. We soon after this became convinced that we could not remain much longer undiscovered, and that we must abandon our enterprise." Samuel Arnold dropped out of the group, Michael O'Laughlin went home to Baltimore, and John Surratt resumed his work as a secret courier for the Confederacy.

John Wilkes Booth never expressed what he felt about the total failure of the kidnapping schemes into which he had poured so much of his energy and resources. But within twenty-four hours he switched gears completely. On March 18, he went onstage at Ford's Theatre for what would be his last appearance as an actor. It was a benefit performance of the melodrama *The Apostate*, with all proceeds going to his actor friend John McCullough. John Wilkes played the villain, Pescara, and got an enthusiastic reception. Newspapers the next day reported that the audience was unusually demonstrative, and showed its appreciation by stamping on the floor and cheering loudly when Booth made his entrance.

Apparently the warm welcome did not make much of an impression on John. At the end of the play, he ignored the crowd's applause and declined to take a curtain call. Meanwhile, in New York, his brother Edwin concluded his triumphant twelve-week run in *Hamlet* on March 22 and left almost immediately for Boston to fulfill a long-standing commitment in that city. He had hoped to take Edwina with him but decided she would be better off visiting her cousins—Asia's children—in Philadelphia.

John took advantage of Edwin's absence to pay a brief visit to New York at the end of March. Since their quarrel following the benefit performance of *Julius Caesar,* the two brothers had tended to avoid each other. During John's New York stay, his mother and June had both tried to get him to resume his acting career. But John refused to listen, saying he still had business to tend to in Washington, including his romance with Lucy Hale.

Bad news greeted him on his return to the capital. In Virginia, General Robert E. Lee continued to defend Richmond, but his 50,000 Confederate soldiers were no match for Ulysses S. Grant's Union army of 120,000 men, with more in reserve. If that wasn't bad enough, General Sherman's Union

General Ulysses S. Grant, commander of the Union army, at the front in northern Virginia.
Photo by Mathew Brady. The National Archives

troops were marching steadily toward Richmond from the south. Everyone realized it was only a matter of time before Lee would have to abandon the capital of the Confederacy. No exchange of prisoners of war could help him now.

John sought escape from the inevitable in drink. He often frequented a Washington billiard saloon owned by John Deery, who later commented on Booth's drinking at this time. "In liquor, of which he could absorb an astonishing quantity and still retain the bearing of a gentleman, he would sometimes flash out an angry word, but it was a hard matter to provoke him to a quarrel. For a period of about a week, he visited my place every day, sometimes in the afternoons, sometimes in the evenings. During that week he sometimes drank at my bar as much as a quart of brandy in the space of less than two hours. . . . It was more than a spree, I could see that, and yet Booth was not given to sprees. . . . He seemed to be crazed by some stress of inward feeling, but only one who was very intimate with him could have told it."

John's mood darkened further after Lee was forced to evacuate Richmond on April 3. As Lee and his battered troops headed west in a desperate attempt to continue the fight, John's behavior became more extreme. Walking along the Potomac with a friend, he looked across the river and moaned "Virginia! Virginia!" in a grief-stricken voice. He talked of mounting his horse and "tearing up and down the streets of Washington, waving a Confederate flag in each hand." But such a gesture would have done little to help Lee and his hungry, exhausted men, who found their escape route blocked in every direction.

The end was not long in coming. Realizing that he had run out of options, Lee sent a message to his Union opponent, Grant, saying he was ready to surrender. The ceremony took place in the town of Appomattox Courthouse on April 9, and in the next few days the remaining Confederate armies followed Lee's example and surrendered also. The Civil War, which had lasted for almost exactly four years and left more than 620,000 dead or wounded soldiers in its bloody wake, was over at last.

Millions of Americans rejoiced at the news of Lee's surrender, among them Edwin Booth. From Boston, he wrote a letter to the widow of a friend who had died in the fighting. "Yes, the news is indeed glorious," Edwin said. "I am happy in it, and glory in it, although Southern-born. God grant the end, or rather the beginning, is now at hand."

But John Wilkes Booth was in despair. He could not accept the surrender of his beloved South, and drank even more than usual. On April 11, John, Davey Herold, and Lewis Powell joined a huge crowd that gathered on the White House grounds to hear Abraham Lincoln deliver a victory speech from a balcony. One passage in the talk focused on the place of African Americans in the newly reunited nation. In it, the president expressed his thoughts on the controversial question of voting rights for blacks. "I would myself prefer that it [the right to vote] were now conferred on the very intelligent [literate blacks], and on those who served our cause as soldiers," he said.

Most of the crowd seemed to react favorably to Lincoln's words, but Booth was furious. "That means nigger citizenship," he said to his companions. "Now, by God, I'll put him through. That is the last speech he will ever make."

Later, in a diary entry, Booth wrote that after spending six months plotting to capture the president, he had reached a point where he realized that "our cause being almost lost, something decisive & great must be done." The realization may have come to him as he stood on the White House lawn that night, listening to the president's speech.

Then, on April 13, Washington mounted a spectacular celebration of the war's end. Orders went out for the major government buildings to be illuminated that night. The main post office had more than 500 lighted candles in its windows, and the huge Patent Office building was ablaze with nearly 6,000 candles. John found all the lights, music, and merrymaking almost impossible to bear. He told a friend he wished the candles would set the buildings afire and burn them all to the ground.

Around noon on Friday, April 14—Good Friday—John stopped by Ford's Theatre to pick up his mail. Like many actors, he had it delivered there rather than to his hotel. As he approached the building on horseback, the brother of the theater's owner turned to some friends and said, "Here comes the handsomest man in Washington!"

In the lobby, John heard that President and Mrs. Lincoln were expected at the theater that night, along with General and Mrs. Grant. As usual, the party would occupy the state box. If he hadn't decided on it sooner, that may have been the moment when John Wilkes Booth decided to assassinate the president—and not just the president, but General Grant also. And

A contemporary engraving shows Satan urging John Wilkes Booth, holding a pistol, to assassinate President Lincoln.
The Library of Congress

that was only the beginning. John went on to conceive an even broader plan, one that—if successful—would fatally cripple the Union government and perhaps pave the way for a Confederate victory after all.

But he would have to move quickly. Within the hour he sent word to Lewis Powell and George Atzerodt, two members of the kidnapping plot who had stayed on in Washington. He said he had new assignments for them, and told them to meet him at eight that evening at the Herndon House, a hotel not far from Ford's Theatre. Then, in preparation for his deadly mission, he set out on a round of last-minute errands.

Meanwhile, the president's plans for the evening had changed. General Grant and his wife bowed out at the last minute, saying they had decided

Ford's Theatre is the large building in the center of this photograph, taken in 1865. Note the sorry condition of the unpaved street. *The Library of Congress*

to go to New Jersey for the weekend instead. After inviting several other couples, Mrs. Lincoln finally lined up a young friend, Clara Harris, and her beau, Major Henry Rathbone, to accompany them to the theater. It was too late for the change to be noted in newspaper listings of the president's schedule, so John did not learn of it. In late afternoon, he rode his horse to a stable in the alley behind Ford's Theatre and left it there, saying he'd be back for the animal later. Still wearing his spurs, he walked five blocks to the National Hotel to keep a date with his fiancée, Lucy Hale.

A woman who knew John saw him and Lucy conversing in a shadowy alcove off the lobby. Then the two of them dined at the hotel with Lucy's mother. Also in the party were an English lady who was visiting Washington and the woman who had observed John and Lucy earlier.

After the last course, John looked at his watch and said, "I must go." He bowed to Lucy and her mother and started toward the dining-room door. But before he got there, he suddenly turned around and came back to the table. He took one of Lucy's hands in his and recited words that Hamlet says to his lost love, Ophelia, in Shakespeare's play: "Nymph, in thy orisons [prayers] Be all my sins remembered." And then, with a smile, he strode out of the dining room. Neither Lucy nor her mother was surprised at his parting words; John often quoted lines from Shakespeare in his conversation.

It was now nearly eight o'clock. John walked quickly from the National to the Herndon House to keep his appointment with Lewis Powell and George Atzerodt. The trio sat in a quiet corner of the hotel's bar while John told the others what he planned to do that night, and gave them their marching orders. Atzerodt and Vice-President Andrew Johnson both had rooms at the Kirkwood House hotel. Before ten thirty, Atzerodt would find a way to get into the vice-president's room and stab him to death. At the same time, Powell would go to the house near the White House where Secretary of State William H. Seward lived and kill the influential cabinet officer. Thus, within the space of an hour or so, four of the key figures in the Lincoln administration—the president himself; his victorious general, Ulysses S. Grant; his vice-president, Andrew Johnson; and his secretary of state, William H. Seward—would all be eliminated.

It's not known how Powell and Atzerodt reacted to Booth's disclosure of his new plan and the roles they were assigned to play in it. Perhaps John had hinted earlier that he had something similar in mind, and so his lethal instructions did not come as a complete surprise. At any rate, the two men seemed to go along with their assignments willingly—especially Lewis Powell—and John proceeded deliberately with his own preparations after leaving them. The performance at Ford's Theatre had started at eight, but John was in no hurry. He wasn't in the cast, so he didn't intend to make his move against the president until the play was well under way.

In the meantime, President and Mrs. Lincoln climbed into their carriage and left the White House at around eight fifteen. They'd been delayed by several last-minute visitors. The president was wearing his usual black overcoat and high black silk hat, and Mrs. Lincoln was dressed in a smart gray silk dress and matching bonnet. The night was foggy, but that didn't slow their carriage. They picked up Major Rathbone and Miss Harris and arrived at the theater at eight thirty. The president's soldier guard for the evening, John F. Parker, had gone on ahead and was waiting for them.

The play they'd come to see was *Our American Cousin,* one of the most popular comedies of the day. Written by Tom Taylor, an English playwright and critic, it told the story of Asa Trenchard, a rough-hewn but good-hearted Vermont farmer who goes to England to claim a fortune he has inherited. The comedy develops from Asa's encounters with his snobbish British relatives, many of whom have not met an American before.

Starring in the production at Ford's Theatre was Laura Keene, the actress who had performed with Edwin Booth years before in San Francisco and traveled with him to Australia and Hawaii. Since her return to the United States, Keene had enjoyed a hugely successful theatrical career, including seven years as the manager of her own theater, the Laura Keene, in New York City. During her time as actress-manager—a rare accomplishment for a woman in her day—Keene acquired the American rights to *Our American Cousin.* She staged it often in New York and on tour, and the play never failed to get a warm response from audiences out for a good time.

That was certainly true of the sold-out crowd in Ford's Theatre the night of April 14. The audience was already roaring with laugh-

Playbill for *Our American Cousin* at Ford's Theatre, April 14, 1865.
The Library of Congress

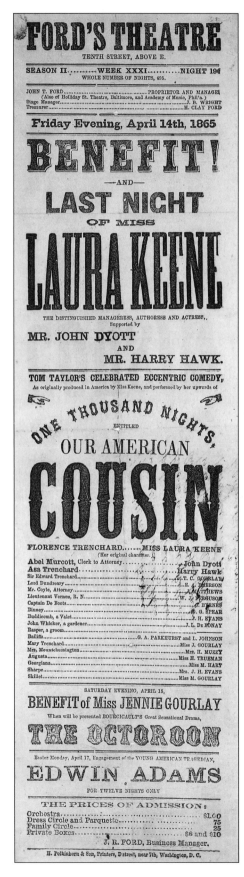

ter when the Lincolns and their guests made a belated entrance at eight thirty-five. As the presidential party took their seats in the state box, Laura Keene, who was onstage in the role of Florence Trenchard, saw them. She improvised a line, "Anybody can see *that*," and pointed toward the box. The audience followed her gesture, spotted the president, and burst into applause. The stage orchestra swung into a rendition of "Hail to the Chief," and Lincoln rose to acknowledge the crowd's greeting. Only after he had resumed his seat in a rocking chair thoughtfully provided by the management did the performance continue.

While Lincoln and his wife settled back to enjoy the play, John Wilkes Booth retrieved his horse from the stable behind Ford's. He got Edman Spangler, a stagehand he knew, to tether the animal near the theater's back entrance. Then he went into the Star Saloon next door to the theater and ordered a shot of whiskey. It was probably in the bar that John learned

Laura Keene in the 1860s.
Photo by Mathew Brady.
The Library of Congress

The stable behind Ford's Theatre, where John Wilkes Booth left his horse.
The Library of Congress

General Grant had not come to the theater with the Lincolns after all. But Grant's absence did not deter John from proceeding with the assassination plot. Lincoln was there, and that was what counted.

At ten o'clock, Booth left the Star Saloon and strolled into the theater lobby. James Buckingham, the doorman, had his back to the entrance and one arm across it to keep people out. John reached out to grasp Buckingham's hand, and the startled doorman swung around. "You'll not want a ticket from me, will you, Buck?" John asked, and the doorman, who recognized the actor at once, waved him into the theater.

John knew every nook and cranny of Ford's Theatre, having performed there on many occasions. He also knew *Our American Cousin,* and had timed his arrival to coincide with a particular scene in Act III. Once inside the theater, he climbed the stairs to the balcony and moved quietly down the sloping side aisle toward the state box. He was in luck, for John Parker, the soldier who was supposed to be guarding it, had slipped into an empty balcony seat to watch the play.

John eased into the small anteroom that led to the box and put a bolt through the lock so no one else could enter. Then he peered through a peephole in the door to the box itself. There was the president, with Mrs. Lincoln sitting beside him and Major Rathbone and Miss Harris on a small sofa to one side. All of them were focused intently on the performance. From the stage, the voices of the actors sounded loud and clear. The actress playing Mrs. Mountchessington, an aristocratic matron, was speaking to Asa, the American cousin: "I am aware, Mr. Trenchard, you are not used to the manners of good society, and that, alone, will excuse the impertinence of which you have been guilty!" With that, Mrs. Mountchessington swept off, leaving Asa alone onstage.

This was the moment Booth had been waiting for. He opened the door

The state box in Ford's Theatre. Note the portrait of George Washington at the bottom of the central pole. *The Library of Congress*

Engraving of the moment when Booth fired the fatal shot at President Lincoln. *The Library of Congress*

to the box and, standing just a few feet from the president, drew the derringer from his pocket. "Don't know the manners of good society, eh?" the actor playing Asa was saying. "Well, I guess I know enough to turn you inside out, old gal—you sockdologizing old man-trap!" As the audience, including Lincoln and his wife, erupted in loud laughter, John aimed the derringer at the back of the president's head and fired.

Lincoln made no sound as he slid sideways in his rocking chair, mortally wounded. John dropped the derringer and lunged toward the railing of the box. Mrs. Lincoln and Clara Harris sat frozen in their seats, Clara's dress and hands spattered with the president's blood. Major Rathbone was the first to realize what had happened. He sprang up from his seat and grabbed hold of John before he could jump down to the stage, a number of feet below. John wrenched free of the major's grasp, pulled a knife from his pocket, and slashed Rathbone across the left arm. Before Rathbone could

John Wilkes Booth shouts *"Sic semper tyrannis!"* from the stage of Ford's Theatre in a painting done some years after the event.
The Library of Congress

recover, John swung over the edge of the railing and jumped. But one of his spurs caught on the flag draped over the front of the box.

John managed to yank the spur free, but he landed heavily on his left leg, fracturing a bone just above the ankle. Up till then most of the audience had no idea what was going on. Some even thought the gunshot, and the sudden exit of the actor playing Asa Trenchard, were part of the play. Only after John landed awkwardly on the stage and Major Rathbone shouted, "Stop that man!" did they grasp that something dreadful had occurred. Their fears were confirmed when Mrs. Lincoln began to sob hysterically. But most of those sitting in the orchestra were still too stunned to move.

Relishing his last moment in the spotlight, John raised himself to his full height, and a few audience members recognized him. He fixed his gaze on the state box, brandished the bloody knife, and shouted the Latin words *"Sic semper tyrannis!"* ("Thus always to tyrants!"). Some thought they also heard him say, "The South is avenged!" Then he turned and limped off-stage. William Withers, the conductor of the theater's orchestra, accidentally blocked his path as he headed toward the back door. "Let me pass! Let me pass!" Booth shouted, and he slashed at the terrified Withers, ripping a hole in the man's jacket.

A stagehand moved to stop Booth, but the actor had already gone through the door and slammed it behind him. Before the stagehand could get the door open again, Booth mounted the horse that Edman Spangler had been keeping for him in the alley. He swung the mare onto F Street and raced off into the night. No more than five minutes had passed since he had shot the president. But in those five minutes John Wilkes Booth had become a fugitive assassin.

Engraving of John Wilkes Booth fleeing on horseback from Ford's Theatre.
The Library of Congress

Chapter 13
THE TERRIBLE
AFTERMATH

$\mathcal{S}$HORTLY BEFORE ELEVEN P.M., John arrived at the Navy Yard Bridge across the Potomac's eastern branch. Wartime security was still in effect even though Lee had surrendered, and the bridge was guarded by three Union soldiers. When they asked John who he was and where he was headed, he rather surprisingly gave them his real name and said he was returning to his home in Maryland. Apparently he convinced the soldiers that he posed no threat, for they let him proceed. He urged his mare forward and disappeared into the darkness on the other side of the river.

A little while later, Davey Herold, one of John's accomplices, approached the same bridge on a rented horse. He and John had arranged earlier that day to meet at a certain time and place in Maryland. Herold came from the region and knew all its back roads, which would be extremely useful as John plotted his escape route. Unlike John, Davey gave the soldiers on guard at the bridge an alias, but they waved him on just the same. He spurred his horse and hurried to keep his appointment with Booth.

The other elements in John's bold plot to bring down the U.S. government did not go as smoothly. In his room at the Kirkwood House, George Atzerodt had his Bowie knife at the ready to kill Vice-President Andrew Johnson. As the hour for the deed drew nearer, though, Atzerodt got cold feet. Instead of going to Johnson's room on the floor below and knocking on the vice-president's door, Atzerodt went down to the hotel bar. After drinking there for a half hour or so, he headed out into the street. He found a tavern in the next block and spent the night there, getting more and more drunk as the hours passed.

Unlike Atzerodt, Lewis Powell set out that evening fully intending to

Vice-President
Andrew Johnson.
Photo by Mathew Brady.
The Library of Congress

carry out his assignment—the assassination of Secretary of State William H. Seward. The neatly dressed Powell told a servant who answered the door at Seward's home that he had brought medicine for the secretary. Powell knew that Seward had been seriously injured in a carriage accident a week earlier and was recuperating in bed at home. The servant believed Powell's story and let him in. But Seward's son Frederick was not as trusting. He intercepted Powell on the stairs and told him he couldn't go any farther.

Determined to carry out his mission, Powell pulled out a revolver and aimed it at Frederick. When the gun failed to go off, he pistol-whipped Frederick with it, knocking the young man to the floor. Then, drawing a knife, Powell headed for Seward's bedroom. Two more people tried in vain to stop him: Seward's daughter, whom he shoved viciously aside, and a male army nurse, whom he slashed across the brow. Entering Seward's dimly lit room, Powell crossed to the secretary's bed and stabbed the sleeping man three times about the head. As Seward fell helplessly from the bed to the floor, Powell turned away and lurched out of the room.

Another of Seward's sons, Augustus, and the revived army nurse tried to stop him, but Powell ran down the stairs and out into the street shouting, "I'm mad! I'm mad!" He left behind some important evidence, though—his slouch hat and the revolver that hadn't fired. More important, he failed to achieve his goal. Secretary of State Seward, though badly wounded, was still alive.

While all of this was going on, the audience at Ford's Theatre had emerged from their state of shock. "I have never witnessed such a scene," said Seaton Monroe, an attorney in the audience. "The seats, aisles, galleries, and stage were filled with shouting, frenzied men and women."

Laura Keene, fearing some in the crowd might be injured, strode to the front of the stage. "For God's sake have presence of mind," she said, "and keep your places, and all will be well."

LEFT: Secretary of State William H. Seward. *Photo by Matthew Brady. The Library of Congress* RIGHT: Lewis Powell. *Photo by Alexander Gardner. The Library of Congress*

Major Rathbone opened the door to the box that Booth had locked and allowed two men who said they were doctors to enter. Dr. Charles A. Leale, a young army surgeon, and Dr. Albert King, a Washington physician, had both been sitting in the balcony. They were soon joined by another surgeon, Dr. Charles Taft, who climbed up into the box from the orchestra, where he had been seated with his wife.

The president showed no signs of life, but Dr. Leale and his colleagues attempted artificial respiration. After a few minutes, they detected a faint heartbeat, and then Lincoln began breathing irregularly. Dr. Leale was not hopeful, though. After sticking a finger into the President's head wound to determine how deep it went, the young doctor said solemnly, "His wound is mortal; it is impossible for him to recover."

Clara Harris attempted to console Mrs. Lincoln, who continued to sob uncontrollably. Someone called for water for the president, and Laura Keene, still in her stage costume and makeup, brought a pitcher up to the box. At the doctors' request, a bottle of brandy was brought up also. While Laura Keene held the president's head, Dr. Leale poured a small amount of the liquor into the president's mouth, and he managed to swallow and retain it.

Now those concerned had to decide where to take the president. Major Rathbone assumed he would be transported back to the White House in his carriage, but the surgeons said that would be too dangerous. They were convinced that Lincoln, in his precarious state, would never survive the seven-block ride over the rough, unpaved streets between Ford's Theatre and the presidential residence. Instead, they recommended that he be conveyed to the nearest house.

It may seem odd that apparently no one thought of taking Lincoln to a hospital for treatment. But they probably felt that nothing more could be done for him there than in a private home. The x-ray had not yet been invented, so doctors had no way of judging how much damage Booth's bullet had done to the president's brain. Nor had modern techniques of brain surgery been perfected. Besides, a carriage ride to a hospital would probably have been as risky as a drive back to the White House.

Major Rathbone cleared away the curious crowd that had gathered outside the state box. Then the three doctors, aided by four men from the audience, including John Parker, carried Lincoln out of the box. They went up the

Engraving of President Lincoln being carried out of Ford's Theatre.
The Library of Congress

balcony aisle, down the steep flight of stairs to the orchestra, and out onto Tenth Street. Major Rathbone and Mrs. Lincoln followed the president down the stairs, the major leaving a trail of blood from his arm wound. An army lieutenant who had been seated in the balcony escorted Miss Harris.

Word that the president had been shot had spread quickly, and a huge crowd was assembled outside the theater, waiting for word of his condition. Ten members of the Union Light Guard had been summoned to help keep order. Now the soldiers opened up a space around the presidential party while the doctors decided where to go. Suddenly a young man standing on the stoop of a lodging house across the street called, "Bring him in here!" The president's bearers took the man up on his invitation. They carried Lincoln carefully through the crowd, up the curving front steps, and into the three-story brick house.

The man who had issued the invitation directed the group to a small room at the back of the first floor. A bed occupied most of the space in the room, but it wasn't long enough to accommodate Lincoln's tall frame. In order for him to rest comfortably, he had to be laid diagonally across the bed, with his head resting on pillows placed in a corner near the door, and his feet, still in their boots, in a corner by the wall.

For the next eight hours, Lincoln's doctors did their best to limit the number of people in the room while they attended to the dying president. Mrs. Lincoln was allowed to see her husband at intervals, but, racked by spasms of sobbing, she spent most of the night in the front parlor of the house. Major Rathbone, having done his duty to the president, finally left to get treatment for his wounded arm.

Doctor Leale sent word to Lincoln's family physician, Dr. Robert Stone, and to the surgeon general of the United States, Dr. Joseph Barnes, advising them of the president's condition. The two men arrived at Lincoln's bedside shortly before midnight, Dr. Barnes having come from treating the wounded secretary of state. Lincoln's son Robert was summoned also. He came from the White House, and after nearly breaking down at the sight of his father's discolored face, he went into the parlor to try to console his distraught mother.

Soon afterward, Secretary of War Edwin H. Stanton arrived at the house on Tenth Street and immediately took charge. He telegraphed Ulysses S. Grant in Philadelphia, where he and his wife were staying overnight, and advised him to return to Washington at once. He also notified Vice-President Andrew Johnson that the President was dying, and sent word to the chief justice of the Supreme Court, Salmon P. Chase, that he should be prepared to administer the oath of office to the vice-president on a moment's notice. Stanton also issued regular bulletins to the press on the president's condition, which continued to deteriorate. Around one A.M. the doctors tried to administer a few more drops of brandy to Lincoln, but he was unable to swallow them.

During the night, Stanton launched an investigation to confirm that John Wilkes Booth was indeed the assassin. Testimony was taken from people in the audience at Ford's Theatre who had recognized Booth, from members of the cast of *Our American Cousin,* many of whom knew Booth well, and from several people who said they had seen Booth after he fled the theater. But no reports had yet come in from anyone who had spotted him after he crossed the Navy Yard Bridge.

Lincoln's pulse rate and breathing remained fairly steady through the early-morning hours, but he displayed no other signs of life. He had not opened

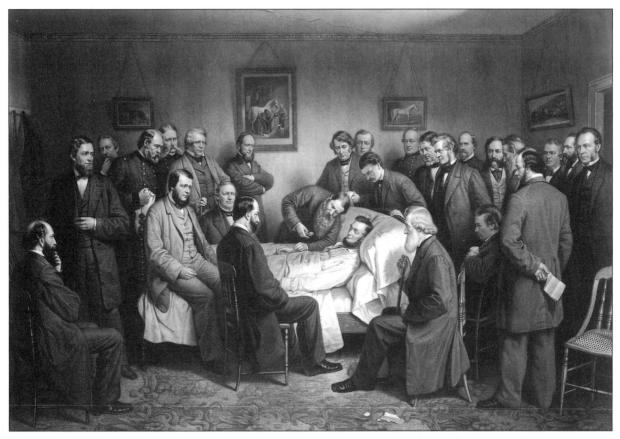

An artist's conception of President Lincoln on his deathbed, surrounded by doctors and members of his government. *The Library of Congress*

his eyes or made a sound since being wounded. Then at six A.M. on Saturday, April 15, his pulse rate dropped and his breathing became extremely labored. The end wasn't far off now. It came at last at seven twenty-two, almost exactly nine hours after he had been shot at Ford's Theatre.

Within a few minutes, the news of Lincoln's death went out to every corner of the United States via telegraph. In the North, the first reaction was one of shock and disbelief. Just yesterday, Northerners had been joyously celebrating the end of the war; now they were plunged into deepest grief at the death of their leader. Lincoln's brutal murder seemed almost inconceivable to most people. No American president up to that time had ever been assaulted, let alone killed.

Ironically, it was Secretary of State Seward—now the target of a near-fatal attack himself—who a year before had expressed how most Americans felt about political killings. "Assassination is not an American practice or habit," Seward had said in 1864. "And one so vicious and desperate cannot be engrafted into our political system," the secretary added, implying that assassination was one of the evils that Americans had left behind when they had emigrated from the old world. In light of what happened on the night of April 14, it was obvious Seward had spoken too soon.

All the telegraphed accounts of Lincoln's death included the name of his suspected assassin: John Wilkes Booth. This, too, was an occasion for shock, since many people across the country had seen and admired John on the stage. But shock quickly gave way to anger, and a desire for retribution. Before the day was out, anyone who knew or had worked with John came under suspicion. The owner of Ford's Theatre and the cast members of *Our American Cousin* were detained for questioning. "I do not know who shot the president," Laura Keene testified, "but the man who leaped from the box was Wilkes Booth."

The revelation that John was the accused killer was especially devastating to his immediate family. In Philadelphia, Asia, who was five months pregnant, let out a scream when she opened the morning paper and saw the news splashed across the front page. Her husband tried unsuccessfully to calm her.

Later, Asia remembered the packet of papers that John had asked her to keep for him. Together, she and her husband opened the safe in the parlor and removed the packet. Inside it they found the letters John had written the previous autumn to his mother and "To Whom It May Concern"; government bonds in the amount of $4,000; and an assignment to his brother June of the Pennsylvania oil field holdings that John owned an interest in. Fearing that the papers might be considered incriminating evidence, John Clarke decided to turn them over to the United States marshal in Philadelphia.

On the night of April 14, John's brother June was acting at Pike's Opera House in Cincinnati, Ohio. Unaware that anything out of the ordinary had happened, he came down from his hotel room the next morning, intending to take a short walk before breakfast. The desk clerk on duty stopped him with a warning not to go outside. When June asked why, the clerk told him of the tragic events in Washington and pointed through the front window

Junius Brutus Booth Jr.
The National Archives

to a crowd gathering in the street. Nervously, the man suggested that June return to his room for safety's sake. June took the clerk's advice, and a few moments later an angry mob of several hundred men stormed into the hotel lobby.

"They would have hanged him [Booth] in a minute if they could have laid their hands on him," the desk clerk told reporters later. Instead, the hotel manager persuaded the crowd to disperse. June spent the weekend hiding out in his room, and on Monday the staff managed to smuggle him out of the hotel. He went to the railroad station, where he caught an afternoon train to Philadelphia. His plan: to ride out the storm at Asia's home.

John's mother and his sister Rosalie got the terrible news in New York, where they were living with Edwin. A woman friend found the two women sitting in the parlor with the shades drawn. Outside, a newsboy was calling, *"Extra! Extra! The President is dead! John Wilkes Booth is the killer!"*

"Oh God," Mrs. Booth moaned, "if this be true, let him [John] shoot himself. Let him not live to be hanged. Spare him, spare us, spare the name that dreadful disgrace!"

At that moment, the doorbell rang. It was the postman, delivering a note John had written his mother the morning of the fourteenth, twelve hours before the assassination. The note gave no hint of what he was planning to do later that day; perhaps he had not yet decided on his fateful action. "Dearest mother," he wrote, "I only drop you these few lines to let you know I am well. . . . Excuse brevity; am in haste. With best love to you all, I am your affectionate son ever." The woman friend did not record Mrs. Booth's reaction to John's note, but it must have upset his mother profoundly.

Edwin, as recounted earlier, was performing in Boston when he heard the dreadful news that President Lincoln had been assassinated and John was the suspected killer. After the remainder of his Boston season was canceled, and he himself was cleared of any involvement in the assassination, Edwin took a midnight train to New York to be with his mother. Edwina was still visiting her aunt Asia in Philadelphia.

There's no record of how Booth passed his time during the long train ride. If he read any newspapers, he would have found little to ease his mind in their pages. The papers were filled with attacks on the theater—the profession to which Edwin had devoted his life. Many commentators were troubled that Lincoln had been assassinated while watching a play, and used this as an excuse to denounce theaters in general. "Would that Mr. Lincoln had fallen elsewhere than at the very gates of Hell," one writer intoned. Another wrote, "The theater is one of the last places to which a good man should go. . . . [It is] the illumined and decorated gateway through which thousands are constantly passing into the embrace of gaiety and folly, intemperance and lewdness, infamy and ruin."

Edwin would also have had a hard time recognizing his brother John from the way he was portrayed in the newspapers. "Savage Beast," "Monster," "Madman," and "Agent of the Devil" were just a few of the words used to describe him. The papers reported that a massive manhunt was under way to find Booth, who had not been seen since crossing the Navy Yard Bridge two days earlier. Since then rumors had spread that he had been spotted in places as far apart as Brooklyn, New York, and Chicago, Illinois. One rumor even claimed that John had disguised himself as a black woman and was hiding in Washington.

Whatever he may have read or thought about during the trip, Edwin kept it to himself. A group of friends, some of them weeping, met him and his traveling companion, Orlando Tompkins, when their train arrived in New York early Monday morning. But Edwin was "stonelike," one of the welcomers wrote later, and he maintained "an almost frozen silence" on the carriage ride home. He probably sensed he would need all the strength and self-discipline he could muster in order to deal with the pressures to come.

Chapter 14
"Hunted Like a Dog"

*A*s THE WEEK AFTER Easter began, hordes of people were hunting for the president's assassin. Union soldiers, government detectives, private investigators, and informers seeking a reward—all were engaged in the search for John in Washington and the surrounding areas of Maryland and Virginia. So far, though, they had failed to turn up any solid clues as to his whereabouts.

An enterprising reporter for the *New York Herald* was more successful in his investigation of John's background. The reporter had discovered that Booth was engaged to be married to a senator's daughter, Lucy Hale, and the *Herald* treated his account as a major story. "The unhappy lady to whom Booth was affianced is plunged in profoundest grief," the report said. "But with womanly fidelity she is slow to believe him guilty of this appalling crime, and asks, with touching pathos, for evidence of his innocence." Out of respect for Lucy, and her prominent father, the paper did not include her name in the article.

Police investigators also made good progress in tracking down Booth's colleagues in the kidnapping and assassination plots. Edman Spangler, who had looked after John's horse while he was in Ford's Theatre, was an easy catch. He was held for questioning on April 15, released, and rearrested two days later. During a search of John's room at the National Hotel, investigators found letters that led them to Samuel Arnold and Michael O'Laughlin, John's boyhood friends whom he had enlisted in the plan to kidnap Lincoln. Both men were arrested on April 17. They confessed to taking part in the kidnapping scheme but denied any knowledge of the assassination.

On the seventeenth, other detectives went to the Washington boarding house run by Mary Surratt. They had heard that her son John was a friend of Booth's and that Confederate sympathizers frequently met at her boarding house. John Surratt wasn't there; he had fled to Canada. But another conspirator, Lewis Powell, turned up by chance while the detectives were questioning Mrs. Surratt. Powell tried to talk his way out of the situation, but the detectives recognized him as the prime suspect in the brutal attack on Secretary of State Seward. They subdued Powell after a brief scuffle and put him under arrest, along with Mrs. Surratt, who was charged with aiding and abetting the conspirators.

It took longer to track down George Atzerodt. After recovering from his binge on the night of the assassination, he checked out of the Kirkwood House hotel and went to the home of a cousin in Germantown, Maryland. But he left behind some items in his hotel room that linked him to Booth, and these, coupled with information gathered from friends of Atzerodt's, eventually led police to his cousin's house. There Atzerodt was apprehended while still in bed on the morning of April 20.

The chief object of the police search, John Wilkes Booth, remained at large. While his pursuers were arresting many of his fellow conspirators, Booth and Davey Herold were hiding out in the Maryland woods only a few miles from Washington. The two men had met in Maryland as arranged on the night of the assassination, but they could not proceed with John's original escape plan because of the leg injury he had suffered. Instead, they headed that night for the home of Dr. Samuel Mudd, whom John had met the fall before when he had toured southern Maryland, scouting routes for his kidnapping scheme.

Booth and Herold arrived at Mudd's house at four A.M. on April 15. Later, Dr. Mudd would claim that he had never seen Booth before, but he did not deny that he prepared a splint for John's leg and made a simple crutch for him. He also fed Booth and Herold and allowed the two men to rest in his house while he went on an errand to a nearby town. There the doctor encountered a Union army troop and learned that John Wilkes Booth had shot and killed President Lincoln. But Mudd said nothing to the army men about the "stranger" he had treated that morning.

On his return home, Doctor Mudd later said, he saw the injured Booth and Davey Herold riding away from his house. That may not have been the whole truth. Perhaps Mudd met with Booth and Herold before they left and warned them that Union soldiers were in the nearby town and were looking for them. At any rate, John and Davey took pains to skirt the town as they rode south toward their next destination, the home of a well-known Confederate agent, Colonel Samuel Cox.

On the way, they had to cross the treacherous Zekiah Swamp. As their horses made their way slowly through the mud and marsh grass, pain shot through Booth's injured leg and he had to stop frequently to rest. The two men finally arrived at Colonel Cox's house a little after midnight on April 16. They did not hesitate to make themselves known to the colonel, and he invited them in to eat and rest until just before dawn. Then, fearing Union soldiers might come to search the house, Cox had his foreman take them to a pine thicket at the edge of his estate. There they could hide until they were ready to move on.

Later that morning, Cox arranged to have another Confederate sympathizer, Thomas Jones, go to the thicket and offer his services to Booth and Herold. For the next five days, Jones looked after the two fugitives. He brought them bedding and food and drink while John rested and tried to regain his strength. This was difficult out in the open with only a crude shelter to shield him and Herold from the chill winds and frequent spring showers.

Each morning Jones also brought Booth the latest newspapers. John was eager to see how they were covering Lincoln's assassination, but he was disheartened by what he read. He had fully expected to be hailed as a hero by the people of the South and by those in the North—and there were many—who had denounced the president and his policies. The opposite had occurred instead: John was portrayed in all the papers as a vicious murderer, while Lincoln had been raised to heroic stature overnight. Even his former enemies now praised him as a great leader who had sacrificed his life to the cause of national unity and freedom.

Lincoln's funeral was held at the White House on April 19. Six hundred dignitaries, including the new president, Andrew Johnson, filled the East Room, where Lincoln's body lay in an open casket. Following the ceremony, the funeral procession started up Pennsylvania Avenue toward the Capitol. There Lincoln's casket would lie in state in the rotunda for the next two days. A detachment of black Union soldiers led the procession, and more than four thousand black citizens followed it, mourning the man who had abolished slavery.

On April 20, while thousands of grief-stricken men, women, and children filed solemnly past Lincoln's open casket in the Capitol rotunda, Secretary of War Stanton offered rewards totaling $100,000 for the capture of John Wilkes Booth, Davey Herold, and John Surratt. The reward for Booth, "The murderer of our late beloved president," was $50,000. Under the actor's picture on the poster announcing the rewards was a brief description: "Booth is Five Feet 7 or 8 inches high, slender build, high forehead, black hair, black eyes, and wears a heavy black moustache."

As the poster was distributed throughout the Washington area, John and Davey Herold were about to make their next move. Thomas Jones, who had been caring for the two men, said the coast was clear for them to try to get across the Potomac to Virginia on the night of the twentieth. Under cover of darkness, the fugitives rode their horses to the riverbank, which was not far from the thicket where they had been hiding. With the help of Jones and Herold, Booth got down from his horse and climbed painfully into a skiff that Jones had concealed among the reeds. It's not clear what Booth's ultimate destination was; so far as is known, he

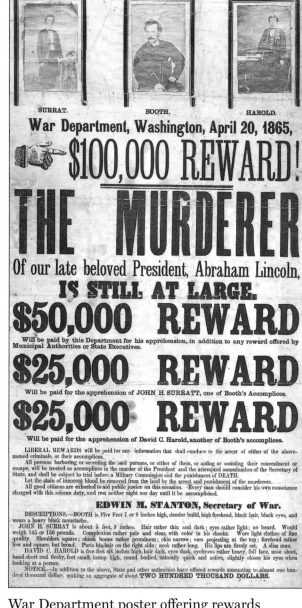

War Department poster offering rewards for the apprehension of John Wilkes Booth, John Surratt, and Davey Herold.
The Library of Congress

never told anyone. But chances are he was headed for Richmond, where he had many friends from his acting days—friends he could count on to shelter him until his leg healed.

Herold rowed the skiff out into the river and headed for the far shore. But something—either the incoming tide or the need to avoid two patrolling gunboats—forced them off course. Instead of reaching Virginia, they landed back in Maryland the next morning, a few miles upriver from where they had started. Luckily for them, Davey Herold knew this part of Maryland well and recognized that they were near the farm of Peregrine Davis, another Confederate supporter. Davis's son-in-law, John J. Hughes, provided the two men with food and a place to rest until sunset, when they would try again to cross the Potomac.

While he waited on April 21, John scribbled a diary entry in the small pocket notebook he always carried with him. "After being hunted like a dog through swamps, woods, and last night being chased by gun boats till I was forced to return wet, cold and starving, with every man's hand against me, I am here in despair," he wrote. "And why? For doing what Brutus was honored for, what made [William] Tell a Hero. And yet I for striking down a greater tyrant that they ever knew am looked upon as a common cutthroat."

He continued in the same passionate vein. "I hoped for no gain. I knew no private wrong. I struck for my country [the Confederacy] and that alone. . . . Yet now behold the cold hand they extend me." (He seems to be referring here to the newspaper stories he'd read that reported the assassination was condemned almost as strongly in the South as in the North.) "So ends all. For my country I have given up all that makes life sweet and Holy, brought misery on my family, and am sure there is no pardon in Heaven for me since man condemns me so."

At the close of the entry, he returned to his immediate situation. "Tonight I will once more try the river with the intent to cross. . . . I do not repent the blow I struck. I may before God but not to man. . . . Who, who can read his fate? God's will be done. I have too great a soul to die like a criminal. Oh may He, may He spare me that and let me die bravely."

The day that John wrote his diary entry, Lincoln's casket was removed from the Capitol in Washington and taken in another procession to the railroad station. A soldier in the procession carried the torn flag that had caught Booth's spur when he'd leaped from the state box at Ford's Theatre.

At the station, an honor guard loaded the president's casket aboard a nine-car funeral train. It would bear Lincoln slowly back to his home in Springfield, Illinois, following the same 1,662-mile route he had taken as the newly elected president in 1861. Along the way, the train would stop in cities large and small so that people could pay their final respects to the martyred leader.

As Lincoln's train moved north, John and Davey Herold made their second attempt to cross the Potomac. This time they succeeded, landing near Machodoc Creek, where a number of Confederate supporters had been told to expect them. One of these was Thomas Harbin, whom John had recruited for the kidnapping plot the previous November. Then, Harbin was to help guide Booth and the captive president through northern Virginia on their way to Richmond; now, Booth needed Harbin to help him and Herold make their escape.

Harbin took the two fugitives to the home of another agent, William Bryant, who supplied them with food and horses. Bryant then led them on to yet another Confederate loyalist, Dr. Richard Stewart, who owned a large house a few miles inland from the Potomac. Before parting company with Bryant, Booth and Herold handed over the horses they had borrowed from him.

Booth hoped Dr. Stewart would be able to treat his injured leg, which was badly swollen, but the doctor did not want to risk getting into trouble with the Yankee soldiers who had moved into the area at the end of the war. He refused to provide Booth with medical care or shelter, and only grudgingly let him and Herold into the kitchen to get some food.

Booth was deeply insulted by Stewart's lack of generosity. He had expected a warmer reception from a Southern gentleman, not to mention an agent of the Confederacy. The doctor directed Booth and his companion to the cabin of a tenant farmer, where Stewart said they could spend the night. As soon as he got to the cabin, Booth tore a sheet of paper from his pocket notebook and penned what he intended as an equally insulting thank-you note to Dr. Stewart.

"Dear sir," it began. "Forgive me, but I have some little pride. I hate to blame you for your want of hospitality: you know your own affairs. I was sick and tired, with a broken leg, in need of medical advice. I would not have turned a dog from my door in such a condition. However, you were kind enough to give me something to eat, for which I not only thank you, but on account of the reluctant manner in which it was bestowed, I feel bound to pay for it. . . . Be kind enough to accept the enclosed two dollars and a half (though hard to spare) for what we have received. Yours respectfully, The Stranger."

The next morning the tenant farmer's son Charley delivered the note by hand to Dr. Stewart's house. On his return to the cabin, Charley agreed—for the sum of twenty dollars—to transport Booth and Herold in his wagon to their next stop, the village of Port Conway on the banks of the Rappahannock River. The journey south to Port Conway took a little more than two hours. When Booth and Herold finally got there just before noon on April 24, Herold looked up a man he knew, William Rollins. He hoped that Rollins would be able to row him and Booth across the river, but Rollins and his young wife, Betsy, had other plans for the afternoon. Rollins suggested they take the ferry instead.

While Booth and Herold waited on the riverbank for the ferry, three young Confederate soldiers rode up to the dock. They had recently been discharged from the army and were on their way home. Herold struck up a conversation with the soldiers, and they promised to help him and Booth find refuge after they reached the other side. Just before the ferry left the dock, Betsy Rollins happened to look out her kitchen window and recognized one of the three soldiers, Willie Jett. She also noticed the crippled man who was standing near Willie. Wasn't he the same man she'd seen talking with her husband earlier?

That day, April 24, Abraham Lincoln's casket was aboard another ferry, crossing the Hudson River from Jersey City to New York. Upon arrival, the casket was loaded onto a hearse drawn by sixteen pure-white horses decked out in black harnesses. The hearse, followed by floats decorated with floral tributes to the fallen president, made its way slowly up Broadway to City Hall, where the President's body would lie in state. That day and the next, thousands upon thousands of New Yorkers young and old lined up outside City Hall to pay their last respects to Lincoln.

Edwin Booth was not among them. Although he had been cleared by the authorities in Boston, the New York police watched his every move and kept him under virtual house arrest in his home on Nineteenth Street. With Edwina still in Philadelphia, and his mother steeped in her own private grief, Edwin would have been terribly lonely if his friend Tom Aldrich hadn't volunteered to stay with him. Some evenings the two men went out for a brief walk after dark. They kept to the shadows to avoid the curious stares of passersby, and Edwin talked of better days when he was full of ambition and had bright hopes for the future. He also speculated on the fate of his brother John. The newspapers were full of accounts of the hunt for John, but so far all the reported sightings had proved false.

Meanwhile, in Virginia, John, Davey Herold, and the three Confederate soldiers had reached Port Royal on the southern shore of the Rappahannock River, opposite Port Conway. Now they were riding two to a horse toward the town of Bowling Green, ten miles farther south. Willie Jett, the soldier Betsy Rollins had recognized, had a girlfriend in Bowling Green whom he was eager to see again. The other soldiers told Davey Herold about a widow named Martha Carter who lived near Bowling Green and operated a sort of brothel with her four daughters. Davey was intrigued—it had been a long time since he'd enjoyed female companionship—but he reminded the soldiers that they had promised to find a safe place for John to hide.

Willie Jett knew a man named Richard Garrett whose farm was just off the road to Bowling Green. The party headed there, and Jett asked Mr. Garrett to let John stay at the farm and rest before continuing on. Jett said he'd be back for his friend the next day. Because Jett wasn't sure of Garrett's political views, he introduced John as James W. Boyd, and when Garrett looked questioningly at John's bandaged leg, Jett explained that he'd been wounded in one of the last skirmishes of the war. At last Garrett agreed to take John in, and Davey Herold helped Booth down from his horse and into the house. Then Jett, his two fellow Confederates, and Davey rode on toward Bowling Green in pursuit of their various pleasures.

That evening John, alias James Boyd, enjoyed a good meal and chatted amiably with Lucinda Holloway, a teacher who boarded with the Garretts. That night he slept between clean sheets for the first time in ten days. John might have been tempted to think his luck had turned, but in fact he was only experiencing a brief lull before the final storm.

Chapter 15
"USELESS, USELESS"

WHILE JOHN WAS CHATTING with Lucinda Holloway at the Garrett farm, a troop of Union cavalry was moving south along the Rappahannock River road toward Port Conway. The soldiers asked everyone they met if they'd seen two men traveling together, one of whom was crippled.

The Union troop spent the night along the road and arrived in Port Conway around noon on April 25. That afternoon they went systematically from house to house in the town. They told the residents they'd received reports that the assassin John Wilkes Booth and his accomplice Davey Herold were in that part of Virginia. Had anyone seen two men who fit their descriptions?

Eventually the troop reached the home of William Rollins and his wife Betsy. Yes, the Rollinses said, they'd seen two such travelers the day before, and one of them had an injured leg. In fact, the men had asked Mr. Rollins to row them across the Rappahannock. Betsy Rollins added that a little while later she'd noticed the two men on the ferry dock, chatting with three Confederate soldiers. She volunteered that she knew one of the soldiers, Willie Jett. Then the ferry had come, the five men got aboard, and that was the last she saw of them.

Did she have any idea where Willie Jett might be headed? the lieutenant in command of the troop asked. Bowling Green, Betsy Rollins guessed. She'd heard that Willie was going with a young lady named Izora Gouldman, whose father owned the Star Hotel in Bowling Green. At last the cavalrymen had something solid to go on. If Willie Jett had indeed gone to Bowling Green, Booth and Herold might have gone with him. Even if they hadn't, Jett might know where they could be found. After thanking the Rollinses for their help, the troop mounted their steeds and rode to the ferry.

Earlier that day, Davey Herold and two of the Confederate soldiers said goodbye to Willie Jett in Bowling Green. Willie had decided to stay on at the Star Hotel with Izora Gouldman and her family. Davey and his Confederate friends rode north the way they had come, Davey to rejoin Booth at the Garrett farm and the others to return to their homes in western Virginia. All went according to plan until the Confederate soldiers, having dropped off Davey, reached Port Royal. As they rode toward the ferry slip, they were startled to see a large number of Union soldiers gathered near the dock. It was the cavalry troop that had interrogated William and Betsy Rollins a short while before.

It's not clear why the sight of the Union cavalrymen alarmed the Confederates so much; Lee had surrendered, after all, and the war in Virginia was over. Perhaps the two young soldiers overheard the Union men talking about their hunt for Booth. In any event, the two Confederates swung their horses around and rode back to the Garrett farm. Arriving at dusk, they warned John and Davey that a Union cavalry troop was on the way and might cause trouble for them. Then the Confederates rode off into the twilight.

John and Davey, who had been resting on the front porch, didn't waste any time. Gathering up their few possessions, they fled into the woods that surrounded the farm. Mr. Garrett, watching from a front window, wondered what was going on. What had the soldiers told Mr. Boyd and his friend that made them run and hide? A few minutes later, he had his answer, when a troop of Union cavalrymen thundered down the road past the farm. He thought they might stop, but instead they raced on in the direction of Bowling Green.

Booth and Davey Herold lingered for a while in the woods before returning to the house. When they did, Mr. Garrett was waiting for them. There's no record of the men's conversation, but apparently the farmer's suspicions about Booth had been aroused. He didn't tell John and Davey to leave, but he did refuse to let them back into the house. They would have to bed down for the night in the tobacco barn, he said. And to make sure they didn't try to steal any of his horses, he had his son padlock the barn door after them.

There's no way of knowing how John reacted to Mr. Garrett's suspicions. But it's safe to assume he felt insulted, as he had with Dr. Stewart.

It was almost midnight when the Union cavalry troop rode into Bowling Green and surrounded the Star Hotel. They found Willie Jett asleep in a room on the second floor. After dragging him out of the bed he shared with Izora Gouldman's brother, they put a Colt Army .44 to his head and got him to talk. Yes, he'd met the crippled man named Booth, Jett said. Moreover, he knew where Booth was staying. If the soldiers would remove the gun from his head, he'd be glad to lead them there.

The cavalry troop, with Jett in tow, arrived at the Garrett farm shortly before two A.M. on April 26. The Union soldiers encircled the farmhouse, then banged on the front door to rouse the owner. A frightened Richard Garrett opened the door in his nightshirt and stuttered badly when he tried to answer the soldiers' questions. Impatient, the army men yanked Garrett out into the yard and shoved him over to a tree, where a thick rope had been flung over a branch. They commanded Garrett to talk or hang, but the threat only made the poor man stutter more.

Garrett's son Jack saved the day for his father. Rushing into the yard, the young Garrett told the soldiers the men they were looking for were locked in the barn. The soldiers immediately surrounded the building. Then they ordered Jack Garrett to unlock the door, go inside, and bring out Booth and Herold. Shaking with fright, the young man did as he was told, but when he came out of the barn, he was alone. Booth had refused to budge.

Now the lieutenant in command of the troop took charge. "You must surrender in there," he shouted. "We give you five minutes."

A crowd looked on silently as the minutes passed. In the yard near the soldiers were Richard and Jack Garrett. On the porch the women of the family, and Lucinda Holloway, huddled in their nightgowns and robes. At the far reaches of the yard, the African-American farmhands stood and stared at the barn.

John Wilkes Booth finally broke the silence. "There's a man in here who wants to surrender," he called. But it wasn't Booth who pushed the barn door open a crack; it was Davey Herold. He blundered out into the moonlit night, hands up, and was seized by three of the soldiers.

The lieutenant called again, this time urging Booth to give himself up. But John had no intention of dying with a noose around his neck like old

Union soldiers lead Davey Herold away from the burning barn on Garrett's farm while another soldier takes aim at John Wilkes Booth.
Engraving from the Library of Congress

John Brown. "Captain," he called in his most actorish voice. "Give me a chance. Draw off your men and I'll fight them singly. Give a lame man a show."

When there was no reply, he called again: "Well, my boys, you can prepare a stretcher for me then."

The lieutenant still said nothing, but he signaled to one of the soldiers guarding the barn. The man set fire to a thick, dry stick and tossed it through the open door. Within seconds the stick ignited a heap of straw inside the barn, and soon the entire structure was ablaze. Those watching could see John through the cracks between the slats. The rising flames illuminated him like footlights on a stage. He was leaning on his crutch with a carbine in one hand and a revolver in the other. As the flames enveloped him, he turned toward the door, and the crutch dropped from under his arm.

At that moment, a shot rang out, hitting Booth in the neck. The soldiers had been told to avoid shooting the assassin so that he could be taken alive and put on trial for his crime. But one of the men had obviously disobeyed the order. For a split second, the stricken Booth gathered himself up; then he fell face-down on the floor of the barn. The lieutenant dashed into the burning barn to drag the unconscious Booth to safety. Other soldiers carried his limp body to the porch of the farmhouse.

A quick examination of his wound revealed that survival seemed unlikely. The bullet had passed through his neck, severing the spinal cord and leaving him paralyzed from the neck down. A soldier poured ice water into Booth's mouth, trying to revive him. The actor spat it up and struggled to speak: "Tell . . . Mother . . . " he began, and then fainted again. He was obviously in excruciating pain, but he came to once more and finished the sentence: "Tell . . . Mother . . . I died . . . for my country."

Soldiers drag the mortally wounded John Wilkes Booth away from the burning barn. *The Library of Congress*

By now the sun had risen and it was getting warm on the porch. Two soldiers started to lift Booth and carry him inside. "No, no!" he said. "Let me die here."

The soldiers brought out a straw mattress and laid John out on it. He couldn't move his arms or legs, but he could still speak. "Kill me," he pleaded, his face twisted in pain. "Kill me!"

"We don't want you to die," the lieutenant said. "We want you to get well."

Lucinda Holloway, the woman Booth had chatted with the evening before, knelt down beside him on the porch. She dipped her handkerchief in cold water and moistened his lips. But nothing could ease his suffering. "Kill me," he begged again. "Please . . . kill me."

The lieutenant and another soldier went through the pockets of John's jacket. Along with a folding knife, a pipe, and a nail file they found his leather-bound notebook. At its back was a pocket containing the photos of five pretty young women with whom John had been involved. One of them was his fiancée, Lucy Hale.

The end was near now. In a faint voice, John asked the lieutenant to lift his paralyzed hands so that he could see them. The lieutenant complied with his request, and John stared for a long moment at them—the hands that had wielded swords onstage, waved greetings to friends, made love to many women—the hands that had held the gun at Ford's Theatre. "Useless, useless," John whispered as the lieutenant let the hands go. They fell lifelessly to the mattress, and a moment later John was dead.

The lieutenant and his men prepared to sew John's body in an army blanket for shipment back to Washington, as was customary for fallen soldiers. Before they did, Lucinda Holloway asked if she might have a lock of his black hair. The lieutenant cut one off and gave it to her.

John Wilkes Booth was dead, but he still cast a dark cloud over the nation. Abraham Lincoln's body continued its slow progress across the eastern United States, reminding people in city after city of Booth's bloody deed. As news of John's death spread, many in the North felt frustrated; they had hoped to see him put on trial and sentenced to hang. A quick death by shooting seemed too easy somehow. Many Southerners, on the other hand, silently mourned the fallen Booth, viewing him as a martyr to their lost cause. The Southerners didn't dare to express their feelings in print, however, for fear of retribution by their Northern conquerors.

Mrs. Mary Ann Booth, mother
of Edwin and John Wilkes.
Courtesy Terry Alford.

Those hit hardest by John's death were the members of his own family. On April 26, as her son lay dying on the Garretts' front porch, John's mother was on her way to Philadelphia to visit Asia, who was ailing. Several days earlier, Asia's husband and her brother June had both been arrested and accused of possible involvement in the assassination plot. The two men had been taken under military escort to the Old Capitol Prison in Washington, and Asia had heard nothing since from either of them.

The arrests were almost too much for Asia to bear, coming as they did on top of a difficult pregnancy that kept her confined to bed. If it hadn't been for her illness, Asia, too, would have been arrested. As it was, she was put under house arrest, and a federal agent was assigned to watch over her day and night. Distraught, Asia telegraphed her mother, and now Mrs. Booth was hastening to her daughter's side.

Launt Thompson, a sculptor friend of Edwin's, rode with Mrs. Booth to the ferry that would take her across the Hudson River to New Jersey. Outside in the street, Thompson heard a newsboy yell, *"Extra! Extra!"* and he glimpsed a giant headline reading "DEATH OF JOHN WILKES BOOTH!" He yanked down the curtain on the carriage window before Mrs. Booth could see the headline. But when they reached the railroad station in

Jersey City, Thompson realized he could no longer keep the news from her. After settling Mrs. Booth in her seat on the Philadelphia train, he hurried to buy one of the afternoon papers. Returning, he handed her the paper, saying: "You will now need all your courage. The paper in your hand will tell you what, unhappily, we must all wish to hear. John Wilkes is dead."

Mrs. Booth, her face heavily veiled, betrayed no emotion when she unfolded the newspaper. Nor did she say anything except "Thank you" and "Goodbye" as Thompson left her and walked toward the exit. From behind him came the excited voices of the other passengers in the crowded car. The one topic in all their conversations was the capture and death of Booth. Some called it God's will. Others were angry, saying they had wanted to see the villain hang! Thompson could only guess what Mrs. Booth must be feeling as she read in silence the detailed account of her son's last moments.

Asia was resting in bed in Philadelphia, awaiting the arrival of her mother, when an elderly employee of her husband's came to the house and asked to see her. The federal guard allowed him to enter, and as soon as Asia saw the man standing nervously by the center table in her room, she guessed what he had come to tell her.

"Is it over?" she asked.

"Yes, madam," the man said without raising his eyes.

"Taken?"

"Yes."

"Dead?"

"Yes, madam."

Her heart beat like strong machinery, Asia wrote later, but she did not cry. She lay back down, her face to the wall, and thanked God silently that her beloved brother had been spared further suffering. Behind her, the old man sobbed as he left the room.

It's not recorded how Edwin Booth reacted to the news of John's death. But while John was still on the run, Edwin had written Asia, "Think no more of him as your brother; he is dead to us now, as he soon must be to all the world, but imagine the boy you loved to be in that better part of his spirit, in another world." And on April 27, the day after John died, Edwin wrote a friend, "At last the terrible end is known—fearful as it is, it is notwithstanding a blessed relief."

Like other family members, Edwin was grateful that John had escaped imprisonment, trial, and the inevitable sentence of death by hanging. But John's death did not bring an end to Edwin's personal problems. He remained under virtual house arrest in New York, and he sorely missed Edwina, who was still in Philadelphia with her aunt and grandmother.

He also had to think about his own future, which was very much in doubt. Ever since the assassination, he had received a steady stream of hate mail like the following anonymous letter: "You are advised to leave this city [New York] and this country forthwith. Your life will be the penalty if you tarry 48 hours longer. Revolvers are already loaded with which to shoot you down. . . . Herein you have due warning. Lose no time in arranging your departure. We hate the name of Booth." The letter was signed, "Outraged Humanity."

Edwin responded to the hate-mail campaign by taking out paid advertisements in the New York, Philadelphia, and Boston newspapers. "My Fellow Citizens," the ads began. "It has pleased God to lay at the door of my afflicted family the lifeblood of our great, good, and martyred President. Prostrated to the very earth by this dreadful event, I am yet but too sensible that other mourners fill the land. To them, to you, one and all, go forth our deep, unutterable sympathy; our abhorrence and detestation for this most foul and atrocious of crimes.

"For my mother and sisters, for my remaining brothers and my own poor self, there is nothing to be said except that we are thus placed without any power of our own. For our present position we are not responsible. For the future—alas, I shall struggle on in my retirement bearing a heavy heart, an oppressed memory, and a wounded name."

Some people and publications responded sympathetically to the ads. An article in the *New York Tribune* stated: "No community could be so cruelly unjust as to allow the stigma of Wilkes Booth's crime to tarnish the fame of so true and loyal a citizen as Edwin Booth." The article went on to say that Edwin's upcoming engagement in New York would no doubt be canceled. But it did not rule out his reappearing on the New York stage at some future date and ended on an affirmative note: "Edwin Booth's friends will not consent to his sharing the odium of disgrace which must be visited upon his wretched and unworthy brother."

The ads did not convince everyone, however. The *Philadelphia Press*, in an editorial, said it could appreciate Edwin's position but felt he would "never be able to go before the public again bearing the name Booth." Perhaps one day he might change his name and then resume his career, the editorial concluded.

If Edwin had hoped the pressures on him would soon ease, he was mistaken. On May 4, Abraham Lincoln was finally laid to rest in Springfield, Illinois, and the newspapers were filled once more with accounts of the villain who had brought the great leader's life to an abrupt end. Six days later, on May 10, the trial of John Wilkes Booth's fellow conspirators began in Washington, D.C. Coincidentally, May 10 would have been John's twenty-seventh birthday.

John Wilkes Booth's body is identified aboard the *Montauk*.
Engraving from the Library of Congress

Chapter 16
DEATH BY HANGING

WHILE THEY AWAITED TRIAL, John's fellow conspirators were held at three different locations in Washington. Dr. Samuel Mudd and the boardinghouse keeper, Mary Surratt, occupied cells at the Old Capitol Prison, while Davey Herold, Lewis Powell, Michael O'Laughlin, Edman Spangler, and George Atzerodt were confined on two ironclad warships, the *Montauk* and the *Saugus*. Those imprisoned aboard the *Montauk* did not know that their leader's body was, for a time, on the same ship. After his death in Virginia, John Wilkes Booth's corpse was transported by horse and wagon to the Potomac, and by boat up the river to Washington. There it was positively identified by federal officials.

Everyone who dealt with Booth's body was sworn to secrecy, but somehow word reached Lucy Hale that her fiancé's remains lay in a cabin on the *Montauk*. Making use of her father's connections, Miss Hale managed to get aboard the vessel, accompanied by two naval officers. She let out a shriek when the covering was pulled back and she saw John's pale face. Overcome by grief, she fell across his body and began to sob. The naval officers raised her, still sobbing, to her feet and led her away.

After an autopsy was performed, a decision had to be made about the disposal of John's body. Secretary of War Stanton feared it might be used as an excuse to resume fighting if it fell into Confederate hands. To prevent any chance of that happening, the corpse was taken, under cover of darkness, to the Old Arsenal Penitentiary. There it was stuffed inside a long wooden gun case and buried under the dirt floor of an empty storage room. Only Secretary Stanton had a key to the room.

Stanton was also in charge of preparations for the trial of the surviving conspirators. Normally these would have been handled by a judge in a civil court, but President Johnson, along with Secretary Stanton and Attorney General James Speed, had insisted that the conspirators have a military trial. They argued that the assassination of President Lincoln and the attempted assassination of Secretary of State Seward were acts of war committed during an armed rebellion. Consequently, the conspirators not only could but should be tried by a military tribunal.

Many respected newspapers, including the *New York Herald,* and many legal experts, including former attorney general Edward Bates, questioned the legality of this procedure. In a letter to the president, Bates stated his position in the strongest possible terms: "Such a trial is not only unlawful, but it is a gross blunder in policy: It denies the great, fundamental principle, that ours is a government of *Law,* and that the law is strong enough to rule the people wisely and well; and if the offenders be done to death by that tribunal, however truly guilty, they will pass for martyrs with half the world."

President Johnson and Secretary Stanton would not be swayed, however, and plans for the military tribunal went forward. Meanwhile, Secretary Stanton, reflecting the anger and outrage of the nation, was determined to make the defendants' prison stays as unpleasant as possible. They were locked in separate cells and permitted no contact with one another. The men's ankles were shackled to balls and chains, and their wrists were bound by an unusual type of handcuff. The cuffs were linked not by a chain but by a rigid iron bar that kept the men's hands apart and rendered them nearly useless.

Most uncomfortable of all were the tight canvas hoods that all the conspirators were forced to wear while in their cells. Each hood covered the entire head and face and had a cord at the bottom, which the jailers tied tightly around the prisoner's neck. There were only two small openings in the hood, one at the nose so the wearer could breathe and another at the mouth through which he or she could be fed. The prisoners were given coffee, soft bread without crusts, and salt meat at eight A.M. and coffee and more soft bread at five P.M. One of the prisoners, Samuel Arnold, later wrote that his hood made it difficult for him to eat and "caused the most excruciating pain and suffering."

The government would not allow the prisoners to be interviewed by

Engraving of John Wilkes Booth and his fellow conspirators in the plot against President Lincoln. Lewis Powell is identified here as "Payne," a last name he sometimes used. *The Library of Congress*

Lewis Powell. Note the rigid iron handcuffs on his wrists.
Photo by Alexander Gardner.
The Library of Congress

members of the press, but it did engage a photographer, Alexander Gardner, to take portrait shots for the record of the men being held aboard the warships. The prisoners were brought up on deck one by one to have their pictures taken. Their hoods were, of course, removed, but not their all-metal handcuffs, which can be seen in some of Gardner's photographs. He took more pictures of Lewis Powell than any of the others, perhaps to confirm Powell's identity with the various members of Secretary of State Seward's household whom he had assaulted.

Shortly before their trial began, the defendants were all transferred to cells in the Old Arsenal Penitentiary, where a makeshift courtroom had been constructed on the third floor. (This was the prison where John

Wilkes Booth lay buried downstairs, but no one connected with the trial knew it except Secretary of War Stanton.) On May 10, 1865, the military tribunal held its first session, and the prisoners were brought down to the courtroom from their cells. Only then were they asked if they wanted to have lawyers represent them.

The formal trial proceedings began on May 12, when the testimony of the first witness was taken. From the start, the defendants were at a disadvantage. The attorneys they'd engaged at the last minute had virtually no time to consult with their clients or prepare for the trial. They were also hard-pressed to locate and call witnesses for the defense, let alone investigate the long list of witnesses for the government.

The defendants and their lawyers faced nine judges, all of them appointed specifically for the trial by the government. Most of the judges were army generals, and none of them had a background in the law. There was no jury. A simple majority vote of the judges would be enough to convict the accused; a two-thirds vote would automatically impose the death sentence. The defendants had no right of appeal. The verdicts and sentences the judges agreed upon would be final; only the president of the United States himself could revoke them.

Soon after the trial began, Edwin was subpoenaed as a potential witness for the defense. Lewis Powell's lawyer planned to enter a plea of insanity for his client. The lawyer hoped Edwin would help him establish that John Wilkes had such a magnetic personality that he could control the thoughts and actions of his associates. Once that point had been made, the lawyer would assert that Powell was not in his right mind when he did John's bidding and attacked Secretary of State Seward.

Edwin obeyed the subpoena and traveled to Washington for the interview with Powell's attorney. However, the last thing Booth wanted was to give testimony about his brother in a public forum. He always felt uncomfortable about speaking in public unless he was playing a role, and that was especially true now. When the lawyer interrogated him closely about John, he replied truthfully that his brother had never talked with him about his conspiratorial activities, nor did he know anything of John's relationships with Powell and the other defendants.

After hearing Edwin's replies, the lawyer decided the actor would be of no use to his client and dismissed him. Relieved, Edwin made plans to leave Washington as quickly as possible. First, though, he paid a visit to his brother June, who was still being held for questioning at the Old Capitol Prison—the same prison where Mrs. Surratt and Dr. Mudd had been confined earlier. Like Edwin, June had told his interrogators that he knew nothing of John's work for the Confederacy or his plots against President Lincoln. But, he told Edwin, he had no idea when he would be released.

On his way back to New York, Edwin stopped off in Philadelphia for a reunion with his mother, Edwina, and Asia. While he was there, Asia's husband, John Sleeper Clarke, returned home after being imprisoned in Washington for more than a month. He had been detained in the Old Capitol Prison along with June, and the two had occasionally had a chance to talk when they were in the exercise yard.

Clarke had given a sworn affidavit to his jailers that he had had no prior knowledge of his brother-in-law's political activities and had never seen the papers John left in the family safe until he and his wife, Asia, took them out the weekend after the assassination. Apparently the authorities believed Clarke, for he was granted his freedom a few days later.

When he returned to New York with his mother and daughter, Edwin discovered that another member of the family had come under suspicion while he was away. His youngest brother, Joseph, had been on a round-the-world trip with lengthy stopovers in Europe, Australia, and California. Joseph was crossing the Isthmus of Panama on his way home when he learned of the assassination, and the shock of it nearly drove him mad.

Joseph's upset was compounded when his ship arrived in New York in mid-May. Two federal agents were waiting for him on the dock and asked him to accompany them to their headquarters. There they subjected Joseph to an intense round of questioning about his brother John. Only after an hour or more did Joseph manage to convince the agents that, except for several brief, innocuous letters, he had had no contact with John while he was abroad.

Of John Wilkes's immediate family, only his mother and his two sisters, Asia and Rosalie, escaped interrogation by the authorities. But everyone in the family felt the shame and disgrace John's murderous act had brought down on them. Asia expressed her emotional state at the time in the memoir of John she wrote later: "Those who have passed through such an ordeal—if there are any such—may be quick to forgive, slow to resent; but they never relearn to trust in human nature; they never resume their old place in the world."

Edwin revealed similar feelings in a letter to his friend Emma Cary: "I wish I could see with others' eyes; all my friends assure me that my name shall be free and that in a little while I may be where I was and what I was; but, alas! it looks dark to me."

Meanwhile, the trial of John's fellow conspirators dragged on through the rest of May and into June. While it was still going on, Junius Booth was released at last from the Old Capitol Prison on June 22. He left that evening by train for Philadelphia, where Asia and her family waited for his arrival at three A.M. A few days later June wrote in his diary: "I hope to God never again to be thus used in a land having any pretensions to liberty."

The trial of the accused conspirators finally came to an end on June 29, 1865, when the members of the tribunal went into secret session to review the evidence. During the seven weeks the trial had lasted, 361 witnesses had testified for or against the defendants, and the court stenographers had compiled a 4,900-page transcript of the proceedings.

Because the trial was so long and complicated, many of the newspaper reporters who covered it thought the tribunal might take weeks to reach its verdicts. They were surprised when the commission members presented their verdicts to President Johnson just six days later, on July 5. The commission found all eight defendants guilty. Four of them—Lewis Powell, Mary Surratt, David Herold, and George Atzerodt—were sentenced to death by hanging. Three of the others, Michael O'Laughlin, Samuel Arnold, and Dr. Samuel Mudd, received life sentences at hard labor. Edman Spangler, whose only crime had been watching over John Wilkes's horse while he went inside Ford's Theatre, got the lightest sentence—six years in prison.

President Johnson approved the sentences at once, and the defendants received official notification of their fates on July 6. Those condemned to death were also informed that their sentences would be carried out the very next day, July 7, between the hours of ten a.m. and two p.m. This allowed them almost no time to seek reprieves from the president, or even to communicate with family members, friends, and clergy.

The press and public did not seem upset by the swiftness with which the sentences were to be carried out. Quite the contrary, in fact. In an editorial, the *Washington Star* commented that "the announcement of the sentences

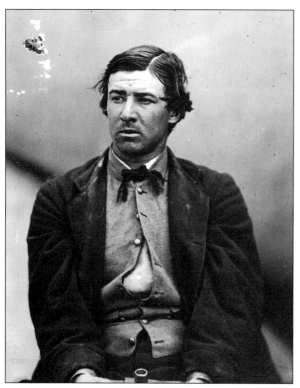

Davey Herold.
Photo by Alexander Gardner. The Library of Congress

Samuel Arnold.
Photo by Alexander Gardner. The Library of Congress

Michael O'Laughlin.
Photo by Alexander Gardner. The Library of Congress

Edman Spangler.
Photo by Alexander Gardner. The Library of Congress

George Atzerodt.
Photo by Alexander Gardner. The Library of Congress

Mary Surratt. *The National Archives*

was rather more sudden than was expected, and occasioned some surprise, though every one approved the dispatch with which the subject had been disposed of." The *Daily Morning Chronicle of Washington* expressed a sharper opinion on its editorial page: "Doubtless there will be some who say, as they have said already, 'but this is too short notice; these wretches ought to have a longer time in which to prepare for their dreadful fate.' Ay! But how much shorter was the time they allowed their hapless victim [President Lincoln] to prepare for *his* fate?"

The death sentences were to be carried out in the courtyard of the Old Arsenal Penitentiary, where work on the wooden scaffold began as soon as the sentences were announced. The hangings would be public, but because space in the courtyard was limited, admission would be by special pass only. "These passes will be given sparingly," the *Evening Star* reported, "no more being admitted than can find convenient standing room."

Curiosity seekers besieged those responsible for issuing the passes, the supply of which was soon exhausted. But that didn't stop those Washingtonians who were determined to see the event for themselves. As July 7 dawned bright and warm, they crowded up to every window in the prison and the buildings around it that had a view of the courtyard. Others packed the rooftops that overlooked it. In a window on an upper floor of the prison, Alexander Gardner and his assistant, Timothy O'Sullivan, set up two cameras to record each stage of the executions.

Shortly after one P.M., the four condemned conspirators emerged from the penitentiary accompanied by their guards and ministers. All the prisoners' overnight appeals to President Johnson had been rejected. One by one, the three men and Mrs. Surratt mounted the steps to the scaffold. They walked with difficulty because of the manacles on their hands and feet. After the four were seated on chairs that had been placed on the platforms earlier, a minister recited prayers for the dying. Davey Herold bowed his head during the reading, while Mrs. Surratt, who was veiled, fixed her gaze on the cross that a priest held in front of her.

When the prayers were over, the general in command of the prison

Standing on a scaffold erected in the courtyard of the Old Arsenal Penitentiary, the condemned conspirators are bound and hooded prior to their execution. Umbrellas shield their handlers from the blazing sun. *Photo by Alexander Gardner. The Library of Congress*

climbed up to the platform and read aloud the order for the execution. Lewis Powell raised his eyes to the sky as he listened. Once the general had finished, guards ordered the condemned to rise. Each prisoner was bound with strips of linen around the arms, knees, and ankles. Then the guards held the prisoners steady as white hoods were pulled down over their heads and nooses were adjusted around their necks.

It was now twenty minutes past one, and everything was ready. The army captain in charge of the execution waved back the crowd of guards, ministers, and attendants that surrounded the prisoners. He clapped three times, and soldiers knocked the supports from under the drops on which the prisoners stood. The drops fell away and the prisoners "were left dangling between heaven and earth," as the *National Intelligencer* reported.

At seven minutes to two o'clock, army doctors examined the bodies of the conspirators and pronounced all four of them dead. A few feet from the scaffold, four graves had been dug earlier in the hard-packed soil of the

The death sentences are carried out and the crowd in the courtyard begins to disperse. *Photo by Alexander Gardner. The Library of Congress*

courtyard. Beside each grave rested a coffin made of plain pine boards. Soldiers cut down the bodies of the conspirators, removed the manacles and bindings, and placed the bodies in the waiting coffins. Other soldiers joined them to lower the coffins into the freshly dug graves and shovel earth on top of them.

"The curtain has fallen on the most solemn tragedy of the nineteenth century," said the *National Intelligencer* in concluding its report on the executions. "God grant that our country may never again witness such another one."

Edwin Booth never commented directly on the trial or the sentences that were carried out on John's fellow conspirators. For the rest of the summer and early fall of 1865, he remained in virtual seclusion in his New York home, rarely venturing outside for fear his appearance might provoke a demonstration. Thomas Bailey Aldrich and other friends took turns keeping a watch over Edwin, worried that he might fall into a deep depression or start drinking again.

By late fall, Edwin had rallied his forces and begun to think again of the future, including a possible return to the stage. His state of mind at this time is revealed in a letter he wrote to Emma Cary: "Sincerely, were it not for means, I would not do so, public sympathy notwithstanding; but I have huge debts to pay, a family to care for, and a love for the grand and beautiful in art to gratify. Hence my sudden resolve to abandon the dreary, aching gloom of my little red room, where I have sat so long chewing my heart in solitude, for the excitement of the only trade for which God has fitted me."

Before making concrete plans for a return to the theater, Edwin fulfilled a request of his mother's. Seven months had passed since the assassination, and Mrs. Booth was eager to reclaim John's body and give it a proper burial. Friends of the Booths had learned from Secretary of War Stanton that John's remains had not been destroyed or discarded, as they had feared, and that the family could have them once the furor over the assassination had died down.

In November, Edwin wrote to Secretary Stanton on Mrs. Booth's behalf. "At the earnest solicitation of my mother," the letter began, "I write to ask you if you think the time is yet arrived for her to have the remains of her unhappy son. If I am premature in this I hope you will understand the motive which activates me, arising purely from a sense of duty to assuage,

Edwin Booth and his little
daughter, Edwina.
*Shaw Collection, The Harvard Theatre
Collection, Houghton Library*

if possible, the anguish of an aged mother. If at your convenience you will acquaint me when and how I should proceed in this matter, you will relieve her sorrow-stricken heart and bind me ever."

The weeks passed, and no reply came from Stanton. Meanwhile, Edwin had decided to return to the stage in January 1866, at New York's Winter Garden, where he had so often performed in the past. For his comeback he would play Hamlet, the role that had brought him his greatest success.

When word got out about his return, Edwin's admirers cheered. But those who could not forget the assassination, and the Booth who had killed their beloved president, were outraged. The *New York Herald* spoke for the latter group on its editorial page: "The blood of our martyred President is not yet dry in the memory of our people, and the very name of the assassin is appalling to the public mind," the newspaper's commentator wrote. "Still a Booth is advertised to appear before a New York audience. . . . Is the assassination of Caesar to be performed? Will Booth appear as the assassin of Caesar? That would be, perhaps, the most suitable character."

As Booth left his home on the evening of January 3, 1866, and rode by horse and carriage to the Winter Garden, he did not know what to expect. Would he be greeted by applause or boos . . . or worse? New York's police department had no idea what would happen, either. A rumor had spread that Edwin would be shot when he made his first entrance, and policemen were stationed inside and outside the theater, ready to deal with whatever transpired that night.

Chapter 17
STANDING OVATIONS

B<small>EFORE THE START</small> of the play, a huge crowd milled about in the lobby of the Winter Garden. Every seat had been sold, but there was a long line waiting at the box office for last-minute cancellations. Standing in the line, some of them grumbling, were many people who rarely if ever attended the theater. They had come tonight out of curiosity, eager to see the brother of President Lincoln's assassin.

Edwin chose not to make an entrance. Instead, as the curtain rose on the second scene of the play (the first in which Hamlet appears), he could be seen sitting in a carved chair amid the glittering Danish court, his head bowed. It took the audience a moment to recognize him. When they did, they rose as one from the orchestra to the topmost balcony and gave Edwin a standing ovation.

The applause and cheers went on for several minutes. At last Edwin rose slowly from his chair and bowed deeply to the audience. When he lifted his head, those sitting in the first rows could see tears in his eyes. The applause continued until Edwin turned to his fellow actors and spoke his first lines. Only then did the audience resume their seats and give their full attention to the play.

When the curtain fell at the end, the audience rose to their feet in another standing ovation. But Edwin and the other actors took no curtain calls. Who knew what madman might be lurking in the crowd, waiting for a moment when Edwin was alone onstage? Instead, he ordered the stage manager to keep the curtain down and light the lamps in the auditorium.

Edwin repeated the policy of "no curtain calls" for the rest of his New York engagement and on the tour of Boston, Philadelphia, and other cities

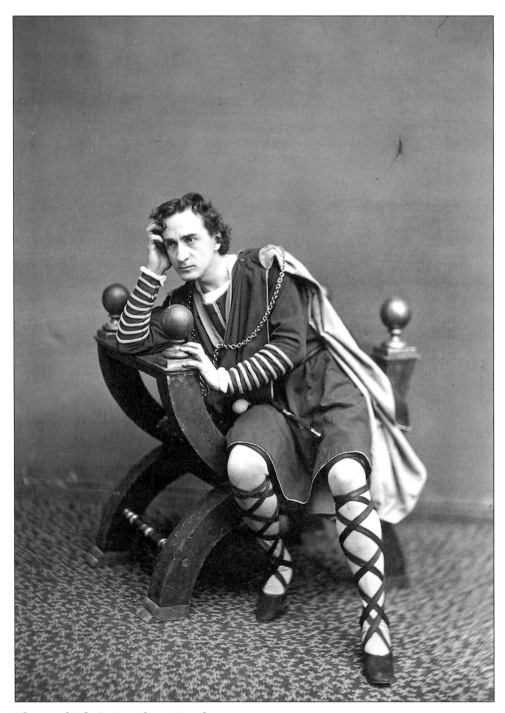

Photo of Edwin Booth as Hamlet. *The Library of Congress*

that followed. Everywhere he went, he played to sold-out audiences and standing ovations. The cheers and applause helped to restore his confidence as an actor and confirmed his decision to return to the stage. However, there was one city where Edwin refused to play, then or in the future. That was Washington, which would forever be linked in his mind with the assassination. If Washingtonians wanted to see him act—and many did—they had to travel to Baltimore aboard a special train that was reserved for theatergoers.

Edwin was back in New York in the spring of 1867, playing another season at the Winter Garden, when the famous old theater caught fire one night and burned to the ground. Gone in the blaze were $40,000 worth of Edwin's costumes, props, and personal effects that he had stored in the building. Edwin didn't dwell on his losses, telling friends he'd experienced far worse. Rather than rebuild the Winter Garden—in which he still owned a part interest—he determined to erect his own theater in New York, the Booth. It would be the finest in the city, incorporating all the latest technical innovations. And on its stage he would present the classics of world theater, enacted by the best available actors amid settings of unsurpassed beauty and grandeur.

Edwin had always known that many elements in society looked down on theater people, considering them little better than rogues and vagabonds. Well, the Booth Theatre would be a kind of beacon, proving that given the right conditions, theater professionals, like him and his colleagues, could create productions of enduring merit.

As his partner in the venture, Edwin engaged a Boston businessman named Richard Robertson. Together they estimated that the combined costs of land and construction for the new theater would be approximately $500,000. Robertson promised to invest $150,000 in the project, and Edwin put down $50,000 in cash to get construction going. Before he left on a demanding tour to raise more funds, he gave his partner a supply of blank checks to fill in as needed.

Edwin's tour took him to Chicago, where he played the McVicker's Theatre, one of the city's largest. Acting opposite him in *Hamlet* and *Romeo and Juliet* was eighteen-year-old Mary McVicker, whose father owned the theater. Booth was drawn immediately to the petite Mary, with her heart-shaped face and curly dark hair. She had a quick wit that amused Edwin and made him laugh—something he had rarely done since the assassination. When he continued his tour, Mary went along with him as his new leading lady.

Edwin had much to occupy his mind these days: the demands of touring, which often saw him playing four or five different roles in a single week; plans for the new theater in New York, the costs of which seemed to rise almost daily; and his developing relationship with Mary McVicker. But much as he might have wanted to, Edwin couldn't forget his brother John and the terrible crime he had committed. Edwin made it a point to reimburse the Virginia farmer whose tobacco barn had been destroyed during John's capture.

Booth also made fresh efforts to obtain John's remains. In the spring of

Playbill announcing the appearance of Edwin Booth and his new leading lady, Mary McVicker, in Shakespeare's *Othello*.
The Harvard Theatre Collection, Houghton Library

1867, he enlisted the help of John T. Ford, whose Washington theater had been taken over by the U.S. government after the assassination. Ford contacted friends in President Johnson's administration but was no more successful in getting an answer than Edwin had been earlier. Later that year, Edwin tried again himself, writing to the new secretary of war, Ulysses S. Grant, on behalf of his mother. "You, sir, can understand what a consolation it would be to an aged parent to have the privilege of visiting the grave of her child," Booth wrote. Once more, he received no reply.

Meanwhile, construction of the Booth Theatre continued through the remainder of 1867 and into 1868. By the middle of 1868, the original estimated cost of $500,000 had been exceeded, the theater was still far from finished, and Edwin's business partner, Robertson, was deluging him with demands for additional money. The pressure soon told on Edwin, and he suffered through many sleepless nights. But he kept on touring—and kept on sending thousands of dollars to Robertson. He also agreed to Robertson's taking out numerous loans in his name.

While Edwin was preoccupied with the construction of the Booth Theatre, his sister Asia was making her own plans for the future. Ever since the assassination, she and her husband had talked of leaving the country. John Clarke had taken the first step, sailing for England in the fall of 1867 and winning recognition as a comic actor on the London stage. Asia and their children followed suit. They booked passage on a ship that left New York for England on March 18, 1868. Asia had told friends she would probably be gone for two or three years, but as things turned out, she never returned to her native land. For her, the very thought of it would always evoke memories of her brother's crime.

In November 1868, Edwin celebrated his thirty-fifth birthday and his nineteenth year on the stage. Three months later, his elegant theater was finally finished, at a total cost of more than a million dollars. The grand opening was set for February 3, 1869, with Edwin playing Romeo to Mary McVicker's Juliet. The next day, the new theater got rave reviews from the critics. They admired the spacious lobby, with its marble walls and floor; the curving staircases that led up to the mezzanine and balcony; and the comfortable plush seats for almost 2,000 spectators. They also praised the production's elaborate scenery and lavish costumes. But they were less impressed by the acting of Edwin Booth and Mary McVicker.

Edwin had never been at his best playing ardent lovers, and his Romeo was apparently no exception. "Mr. Booth knows as well as we do that he can't play Romeo," the critic of the *Herald* wrote. "He seems almost to writhe under the load of sweet fancies . . . when his face should be lit up with a glow of passion it is almost funny to see his struggles to portray the eager impatience of a young lover."

Edwin's leading lady fared no better at the hands of the *Herald's* critic. "Miss Mary McVicker, for whom Mr. Booth gallantly sacrificed himself, we are pained to say is in no way worthy of the sacrifice," the critic wrote. "She is not a delicate geranium . . . but a strong, practical Western woman, with but little artistic training but a good deal of raw vigor and force; and while she can never realize the graceful, buoyant, lovely Juliet of Shakespeare's creation, we have no doubt she would manage Romeo's business after marriage with considerable effect."

Edwin did not let the critics' words sway his belief in Miss McVicker's talent or the strong feelings he had developed for her. Quite the opposite, in fact. While they were acting together in New York, Edwin asked her to marry him. She accepted at once, and they decided to have the wedding in early June, after the theater season was over.

Meanwhile, Edwin made yet another attempt to recover his brother John's remains. In early February 1869, shortly after the opening of his theater, Edwin wrote to President Johnson, and this time he received a reply. The president was about to leave office, and before he did, he wanted to tie up some loose ends. Almost four years had passed since the assassination, and the anger and passion that had surrounded the trial of John's fellow conspirators had long since died down.

In 1867, John Surratt, who had fled to Canada and then Europe to escape punishment, was captured abroad and sent back to the United States to stand trial. Unlike his fellow conspirators, Surratt was tried in a civil proceeding, and when the jurors could not agree on a verdict, he walked out of the courthouse a free man. Now, in 1869, President Johnson decided to free the three surviving conspirators—Samuel Arnold, Edman Spangler, and Dr. Samuel Mudd—who were serving their sentences in the Florida Keys. (The fourth conspirator, Michael O'Laughlin, had died in prison.)

The president informed Edwin that he had also decided to turn John's

A formal photographic portrait of Edwin Booth and Mary McVicker.
The Harvard Theatre Collection, Houghton Library

The Booth family's plot in Baltimore's Greenmount Cemetery, where John Wilkes Booth was laid to rest in an unmarked grave.
The Harvard Theatre Collection, Houghton Library

remains over to his family, on one condition. Those who received the body had to promise to handle the matter with "the utmost secrecy and dispatch, and with the avoidance of all sensationalism and publicity." Edwin agreed immediately to the president's terms, and on February 15 a moving van—

not a hearse, which might have attracted attention—went as directed to the grounds of the Washington Arsenal. Soldiers on duty there raised a pine coffin labeled simply "Booth" and handed it over to the men on the van, who drove with it to the railroad station.

The coffin was put aboard the evening train for Baltimore, where it was received by an undertaker Edwin had hired. Mrs. Booth, her daughter Rosalie, and her son Joseph traveled to Baltimore to identify the body. When the coffin was opened in a back room at the undertaker's, all three Booths looked inside. "Yes, that is the body of John Wilkes Booth," Joseph said as he stared at the mummified remains. John's black hair had grown very long around his shrunken face. Before closing the coffin, the undertaker's assistant snipped off a lock and handed it to John's mother. Mrs. Booth wept as she fingered the strands of her favorite son's hair.

John's body remained in a vault at the undertaker's until June, when everyone in the family could attend the burial service at Baltimore's Greenmount Cemetery. Six local actors carried the body, now lying in a fine mahogany casket, to the gravesite. An Episcopal minister from New York presided over the brief service, after which the casket was lowered into a grave near those of John's father, Junius, and four siblings who had died in infancy. Gravestones identified the plots where the other Booths were buried, but no stone would mark John's final resting place for fear it might be vandalized.

The long road that had taken John Wilkes Booth from a promising career as an actor to the assassination of a beloved president, then to a cruel death on a Virginia tobacco farm, had reached its final destination. His destructive influence lived on in unexpected ways, however. The Episcopal minister who presided over John's funeral had not known in advance whom he was to bury. But when he returned to New York and told his congregation what had happened, they fired him on the spot.

Edwin, on the other hand, seemed to have escaped from his brother's shadow at last. His first season at the Booth Theatre had overcome those first negative reviews and played to sold-out crowds night after night. And on June 7, just three weeks before John's burial, Edwin and Mary McVicker were married at her parents' summer home in fashionable Long Branch, New Jersey. In letters to friends, Edwin sounded happier than he had in years. "My wife," he wrote, "is a quaint, cosy, loveable little body and we get on famously." His daughter liked Mary, too. "She and Edwina are all in all," Edwin noted with pleasure.

At that moment, it looked as if Edwin had gone beyond the assassination and its distressing aftermath, and was on his way to achieving everything he desired most.

Chapter 18
INTO THE FURNACE

The Booth Theatre had become the center of Edwin's life. He involved himself in every detail of the productions staged there, going over costume sketches with the costume designer and checking on the work of the scene painters in the scene shop. He even lived in the theater. The top floor had been planned as an apartment for him, and Booth and his new wife set up housekeeping there. When he left for work, all he had to do was stroll downstairs to the rehearsal rooms or the stage.

Mary McVicker Booth had retired from acting following her marriage to Edwin. She was busy in the early months of 1870, however, preparing for the birth of their child. The baby, a boy whom they named Edgar, was born on July 4 during the middle of a heat wave. It was a difficult birth for both mother and child, and little Edgar's skull was damaged in the course of it. The infant struggled for life but died after only a few hours.

Edwin grieved at the loss of his son, but Mary was devastated. She had always tended to be up one moment and down the next. Now, in the wake of Edgar's death, her mood swings became more pronounced, and she was laid low by one mysterious ailment after another.

Edwin did all he could to help his wife. He engaged the best doctors in the city to treat her, and arranged for her to recuperate in a series of expensive rest homes. In the meantime, he had his own problems to deal with at the Booth Theatre. When he himself played there, he could count on every seat being filled. But many of the other star performers he booked into the theater failed to draw the expected crowds. A half-empty auditorium meant a small profit or no profit at all, and Edwin was forced to take out additional loans just to keep the theater going.

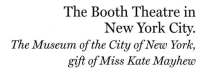

The Booth Theatre in
New York City.
*The Museum of the City of New York,
gift of Miss Kate Mayhew*

By the fall of 1872, Booth realized that he must make drastic changes in the way his theater was run or risk losing it. He bought out his extravagant partner, Richard Robertson, for the then-huge sum of $240,000, and turned to his brother June for help. June offered to lease and manage the Booth for five years, thereby freeing Edwin to tour the country and make the money he needed to reduce the debt load on his theater.

June's plan might have worked if the United States hadn't been hit by the Panic—or Recession—of 1873. Businesses failed right and left, and Edwin's major creditors suddenly found themselves short of cash. They confronted the actor, demanding that he repay everything he owed them. If he didn't, they threatened to foreclose the mortgages they held on his beloved theater.

This time Edwin sought assistance from a smooth-talking lawyer, T. J. Barnett. The lawyer urged Booth to put the theater up for sale. Edwin was reluctant to think about selling the Booth—how could he give up something that meant so much to him?—but in the end Barnett convinced him he had no alternative. The lawyer assured Edwin the theater would bring a good price, enough to pay off the debts the actor had amassed in building and running it.

Resigned to the loss of his theater, Edwin made plans to move out of his apartment on the top floor. But first there was a piece of unfinished business he needed to tend to. One evening in early March 1873, Edwin took aside young Garrie Davidson, who did odd jobs around the Booth Theatre, and asked the youth to wake him at three in the morning. Garrie did as he was told, and Booth led the young man down a narrow stairway to the furnace room under the stage.

Years later, Garrie described to the actor Otis Skinner, who was writing a book about Booth, what happened next. Edwin had Garrie light a gas lamp and stoke the fire in the furnace. Then he told the youth to bring forward a large trunk bound with ropes that was standing in a shadowy corner of the room. Once the trunk was in place, Edwin said, "Get an ax and cut the ropes." Garrie did so, and the sharp odor of mothballs escaped from the trunk when he lifted the lid.

Inside, on top, was an assortment of wigs and stage props—wooden swords, daggers, and the like. The rest of the trunk was filled with stage costumes, all neatly folded and stacked. The trunk and its contents had belonged to John Wilkes. It was the one he had left behind in Montreal in 1864, with instructions to ship it to Richmond, Virginia, where he intended to resume his acting career. The trunk came into Edwin's possession years after the assassination. A friend had bought it at an auction organized by the Canadian government and had given it to Edwin as a gift. But he hadn't opened it until now.

Garrie looked on as Edwin put the wigs and prop swords to one side and brought out the first of the costumes, a blue broadcloth coat. Booth studied the coat from one angle and then another as if visualizing how it had looked when John wore it. Then he handed the garment to Garrie and said, "Put it in there," indicating the furnace.

As the lace cuffs of the coat caught fire, Edwin handed more costumes to Garrie—a Roman toga that John had worn in *Julius Caesar*, Shylock's black robe from *The Merchant of Venice*, a sword belt that had been part of John's costume when he played Iago in *Othello*. Before Garrie threw them into the furnace he noticed that many of the garments had the initials JWB sewn into the linings.

Edwin did not comment on any of the costumes until he came to a long purple shirt, decorated with stage jewels, and a sleeveless, fur-trimmed cloak that was meant to be worn over it. He stared at the garments, then sat down with them spread over his knees. Garrie thought he saw tears in Booth's eyes as he said, "My father's," in a shaky voice. "Garrie, this was one of my father's *Richard III* costumes. He wore it in Boston on the first night I went on the stage as Tressel."

Garrie dared to offer a suggestion. "Don't you think you ought to save that, Mr. Booth?"

"No, put it on the fire with the others," the actor replied. He went back to handing items to his helper and threw some into the furnace himself. At last they reached the bottom of the trunk. "Then we threw the wigs on the coals, and even the swords," Garrie Davidson recalled later. Finally, Edwin told Davidson to break up the trunk and throw the pieces into the furnace, too.

The two men watched the flames devour the last remnants of the trunk and its contents. Then Edwin turned to Garrie. "That's all," Booth said in a low voice. "We'll go now." By then it was almost six A.M.

When they reached the stage, Booth turned once more to Davidson. "Thank you, Garrie," he said. "You needn't come any further with me." And with that Booth strode off toward the stairway that led up to his apartment above the theater.

Why did Edwin feel such a strong need to destroy the last vestiges of his brother John's theatrical career? He never discussed the matter in any conversations or letters that have survived. Perhaps it was yet another attempt to put behind him John's terrible deed and all the pain it had caused the nation, and the Booth family. Or perhaps he simply wanted to clean house before handing over control of the Booth Theatre to a new owner. Whatever his motivation, Edwin obviously decided to keep it to himself.

The destruction of John's trunk was soon overshadowed by more pressing concerns. After eight weeks of effort, Edwin's lawyer, T. J. Barnett, announced reluctantly that he had failed to find a buyer for the Booth Theatre. He proposed instead that Edwin turn over the theater free of charge to another lawyer, who would maintain the property until the economic climate improved and it could be sold. But Booth's creditors were not willing to wait any longer for their money. They refused to renew the short-term loans by which the theater had been financed and demanded immediate repayment.

There was no way Edwin could raise the necessary cash, so his lawyer recommended that he declare voluntary bankruptcy. Booth hated to take this humiliating step, but Barnett persuaded him that he had no other choice. The actor filed the required papers in New York on January 26, 1874, and the newspapers the next day reported that Booth's debts amounted to more than $200,000 while his assets—including his furniture and artworks, and his wife's jewelry—totaled less than $10,000.

Edwin's many friends and associates expressed their sympathy at his plight. His father-in-law, James McVicker, commented, "Had Booth's

Edwin Booth spared no expense on the scenery for his productions at the Booth Theatre, as this set for the play *Richelieu* indicates. *The Museum of the City of New York, the William Seymour Collection*

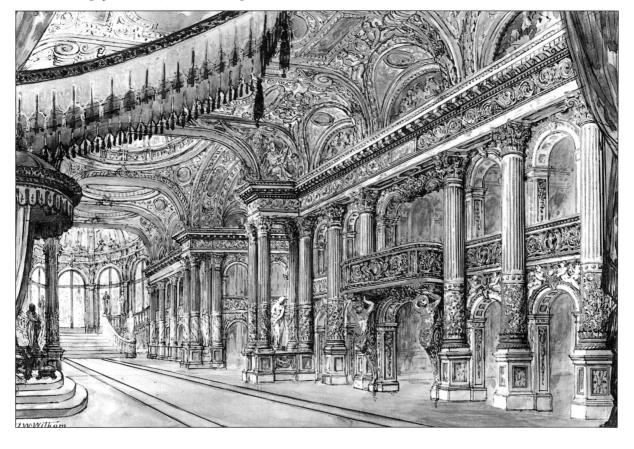

financial affairs been conducted with anything like the ability he displayed in artistic matters, only success would have been the result." The drama critic William Winter echoed McVicker but in more personal terms. "He was a dreamer," Winter wrote of Booth. "The temperament that made him fine in Hamlet unfitted him for practical affairs."

Edwin wrote Winter, thanking him for his support. "It's a terrible blow indeed," he admitted, "but not the worst that I have felt. The loss of money (so long as God grants me the health to work) does not disturb me much; but the fear of being misjudged by my creditors and the disappointment in not being able to establish the true Drama in New York—those are very painful reflections."

Booth was determined to restore his good name with his backers. To that end, he vowed that he would pay back every cent he owed, and set out on an extensive American tour to start fulfilling his promise. On that tour and the ones that followed, he made it a point to write regularly to Edwina, who was now in her teens and away at boarding school. Edwina treasured her father's letters, and later in life she published a collection of them.

In some of his letters, Booth described his impressions of natural wonders like Mammoth Cave in Kentucky. In others, he offered Edwina advice presented in an amusing way:

> *If your lips you'd keep from slips,*
> *Of these five things beware:*
> *Of whom you speak,*
> *To whom you speak,*
> *And how, and when and where.*

Occasionally, in writing to his daughter, Booth revealed his innermost feelings about such things as his lack of a formal education beyond age thirteen. "How often, Oh! how often have I imagined the delights of a collegiate education," he wrote. "What a world of never-ending interest lies open to the master of languages! . . . I have suffered so much from the lack of that which my father could easily have given me in my youth, that I am all the more anxious you shall escape my punishment in that respect; that you may not, like me, dream of those advantages others enjoy through any lack of opportunity or neglect of mine. Therefore, learn to love your Latin, your

French, and your English grammar; standing firmly and securely on them, you'll have a solid foothold in the field of literature."

Booth's wife insisted on accompanying him on his theatrical tours even though she hated traveling. Mary was a mass of contradictions. She had enormous energy and could often outdo bigger and stronger companions, female or male. On a tour of the South with Edwin early in 1876, she hiked thirteen miles over rough country at Mammoth Cave, and followed it up the next day by riding fourteen miles sidesaddle. At the same time, she was full of nervous fears and insisted that she could not sleep on a moving train. Consequently, Edwin had their private railroad car stop for the night on sidings even if it meant delaying or canceling the next stop on the tour.

Touring was no fun in the late nineteenth century, but it could be extremely lucrative for a star like Edwin. The manager of the Southern tour agreed to pay Booth $30,000 for fifty performances. It was the first time he'd acted in the Deep South since the Civil War, and he drew enormous crowds. It annoyed him, though, that everywhere he went, the local newspapers inevitably referred to him as "the brother of the man who killed Lincoln." Moreover, women claiming to have had a relationship with John turned up in many places. One in Birmingham, Alabama, told a reporter that she was John's widow and the mother of his two children. "A damnable lie," Edwin wrote to a friend, and he refused to meet with the woman.

After the Southern tour came to an end, Edwin and his wife headed west for an eight-week engagement in San Francisco in the spring of 1876. This time Booth did not have to take the long sea route to California via Panama. Instead, he and Mary boarded a train on the recently completed transcontinental railroad.

Booth was amazed by how much San Francisco had grown since he had last seen it twenty years earlier. The city's theatergoers gave him a tremendous welcome, filling the grand California Theater to capacity night after night and rising in a standing ovation at the end of each performance. When the receipts of the eight-week run were totaled, Edwin's share amounted to almost $50,000. Adding this to his earnings from the Southern tour, Booth had nearly $80,000 to take home to New York— more than enough to repay the last of the debts on his ill-fated theater.

His credit restored, Booth was discharged from bankruptcy late in 1876.

Family portrait of Mary McVicker Booth, Edwin Booth, and Edwina, now a teenager. *The Harvard Theatre Collection, Houghton Library*

Some of his friends thought he might try to buy back the Booth Theatre, or purchase a controlling interest in another New York theater. But Edwin had learned a painful lesson. From then on, he was content to leave the managing of theaters to others and focus all his energies on his acting career.

As the 1876–77 theatrical season came to an end, Edwin had every reason to be happy except for one thing: Mary's mental state had taken a turn for the worse. She began to suspect people were plotting against her and flew into sudden rages for no apparent reason. Up till then Mary had always seemed to like her stepdaughter, Edwina. But now she snapped at the girl, home from school for the summer, and forbade any mention in her presence of Edwina's mother, Mary Devlin.

In an attempt to ease the tension in his household, Edwin persuaded Mary to spend the summer of 1877 in a sanatorium, where she could get a much-needed rest. She was back home by the fall and insisted on going on tour with Edwin once more. Booth humored his wife, not wanting to set off one of her spells. But over the next several years, his fellow actors often wondered why Edwin let this nervous little woman exert so much control over his life.

Chapter 19
TARGETING EDWIN

WHAT EDWIN HAD FEARED for almost fourteen years finally occurred on March 23, 1879. Booth was playing Shakespeare's unhappy King Richard II at the McVicker's Theatre in Chicago, and was alone onstage for the climactic dungeon scene. Usually he sat on a stool throughout it, but on this particular night he stood up in the middle of the scene and moved to one side.

Booth's impulsive move may have saved his life. For just as he rose to his feet, he heard the crack of a pistol shot, followed by another. Both bullets lodged in the scenery behind him. Edwin looked up at the balcony and saw someone moving in one of the last rows. The man seemed to be getting into position to shoot again. Striding down to the footlights, Edwin pointed a finger at the shadowy figure and shouted, "Arrest that man!" The gunman's neighbors in the balcony responded at once. They surrounded the man before he could fire his weapon and, after a brief scuffle, led him away down the stairs.

Booth's wife had been watching his performance from the wings. When Mary heard the first shot, she began to sob hysterically. Edwin saw her, and as soon as the gunman was subdued, he excused himself to the audience and hurried offstage to reassure Mary that he was unharmed. He returned after a few minutes, sat down once more on the stool at center stage, picked up where he had left off, and finished the play.

Not until the next day did Booth realize how close he had come to being killed. He wrote his friend William Winter that the only thing that had saved him was his unplanned rise from the stool. "[Call it] second sight—

premonition—warning! I don't account for what I did, but there's no other explanation."

The would-be assassin was Mark Gray, who told police he was a clerk in a St. Louis dry-goods store. Edwin had thought the man was probably motivated by a desire to avenge John's assassination of Lincoln, but that was apparently not the case. "It appears he is a frustrated genius," Edwin wrote William Winter. "And because he never knew his father and looks about as much like a Booth as any dark-eyed, dark-haired man might look, he imagines himself to be my rejected offspring. His dates don't tally, however, for at the time of his conception I was at the other end of the world in Australia." Booth summed up Gray as "a lunatic—and a dangerous one," and expressed the hope that the man would be sentenced to life in an insane asylum.

Edwin admitted to Winter that he felt shaky in the aftermath of the attack, but he worried more about its effect on his wife. She was devastated, he told his friend, and woke night after night from terrible dreams filled with guns and bullets. His main concern, though, was his mother. "Think of her and all the horrible past that this event revived," he wrote. "She cannot rid herself of the vision of me lying dead."

Mrs. Booth proved to be tougher than her son gave her credit for. She was living quietly now in Long Branch, New Jersey, with her daughter Rosalie. After the first shock was over, she wrote Edwin a reassuring letter saying she was grateful the incident in Chicago had done him no lasting harm.

His wife was another story. In the late winter of 1879–80, she took ill. "My wife has been gradually wasting away," Edwin wrote Winter. "A severe cough distresses her very much. I've been at times quite alarmed for her. Her will is something wonderful—she won't give up, but—though ill enough to be in bed—she insists on going out as often as possible."

Edwin hoped that a trip abroad would help to revive his wife's spirits. An English producer had approached Booth about performing in London in the autumn of 1880, and the actor was planning to take his wife and daughter with him. They would depart for Europe in the summer so that Edwin could introduce Edwina, now eighteen, to the historic highlights of Great Britain, Ireland, and France.

Edwina responded with delight to the places they visited, and was especially enamored of Paris, where the family spent ten days. But her stepmother could not get over the nagging cough from which she had suffered for months. The Booths returned to London in time for Edwin to begin rehearsals for *Hamlet,* the first play in his season at the Princess Theatre. He also enjoyed a reunion with his sister Asia, whom he hadn't seen since she had moved to England. *Hamlet* opened on November 6, 1880, to polite but lukewarm reviews from the London critics. The *Times of London* called Booth's portrayal "scholarly" and "intelligent," and the *Morning Post* praised him for his "conscientious study" of the role and his moments of "true passion."

Edwin wasn't surprised by the tone of the reviews; he was well aware that British critics believed only English actors could do justice to Shakespeare. "Well, most of the papers 'damn me with faint praise,'" he wrote William Winter, "but at least all acknowledge that I speak good English and do not offend."

Booth got a warmer response when he appeared in Bullwer-Lytton's *Richelieu.* The *Standard's* critic found his performance as the cardinal "from the first to the last . . . striking and effective." Edwin's greatest London success, though, came in January 1881, when he played Shakespeare's King Lear. The *Morning Post* said his performance as the tragic monarch had "touches of beauty and grandeur as pure and lofty as any within the reach of any other actor." By then Booth was attracting capacity audiences to the Princess Theatre, and his London run, which was originally scheduled to end in January, had been extended through March.

Henry Irving was the leading actor on the British stage at the time. Irving was well aware of Edwin's American reputation and had made it a point to read his London reviews. Now he surprised Booth by inviting him to stay on in London after his engagement at the Princess ended and join him, Irving, in a new production of *Othello.* The two stars would take turns playing the leading roles of Othello and the villainous Iago, and Irving was confident they would create a stir.

The proposal intrigued Edwin. It would be a real challenge to match his acting skills against those of Irving, and the production was sure to feature an excellent supporting cast and beautifully designed scenery and costumes. The only thing holding Booth back was the state of his wife's health.

" Thy Name is Great,—We Welcome Thee ! "

Hegger 109 CHEAPSIDE, LONDON.
111 E. 19TH ST., N. Y.   COPYRIGHTED 1883, BY FRANK HEGGER, IN LONDON & WASHINGTON

The eminent British actor-manager Henry Irving (*right*) welcomes Edwin Booth to London in this contemporary cartoon.
Evert Jansen Wendell Collection,
The Harvard Theatre Collection,
Houghton Library

He had taken Mary to a London throat specialist because of her lingering cough, and the doctor had diagnosed the problem as tuberculosis of the throat and lungs. Moreover, the illness had reached an advanced stage.

In the end, Edwin accepted Irving's invitation. He was convinced that Mary was getting the best possible care in London, and besides, she was in no condition to travel. He was also thinking of Edwina, who was thoroughly enjoying her stay in the British capital. "Edwina has the best time of it," Booth wrote a friend. "She has met some very pleasant acquaintances who dine and dance her to her heart's content."

Rehearsals began for *Othello,* and Booth was impressed with Irving as both an actor and a director. "His patience and untiring energy—his good taste and superior judgment in all pertaining to stagecraft, are marvelous,"

Booth wrote to William Winter. "He imparts to the humblest member of his company some of the true artistic feeling that animates himself. Rehearsals are, on his stage, with him as director, positively a pleasure."

Unfortunately, Mary Booth's condition was getting worse, not better. The tuberculosis weakened her physically; she coughed all night and sank into fitful sleep during the day. The disease also affected her mind. She began to think she was being persecuted, and accused Booth of neglecting and mistreating her. Edwina also came under fire. Her stepmother claimed Edwina pinched her hand while she was sleeping, woke her roughly, and made scary faces to frighten her. Booth was so concerned about his wife's physical and mental health that he had the doctors notify her parents by telegraph. Alarmed, the McVickers left Chicago for New York and booked passage on the next available ship to England.

Opening night of the Booth-Irving season in *Othello* was set for May 2, 1881, at London's Lyceum Theatre. All the best seats in the house had long since been sold, and some theatergoers who were accustomed to sitting downstairs in the orchestra had to settle for seats in the last rows of the balcony. Many important figures in London's literary and art worlds were in the audience, including the young playwright Oscar Wilde. Edwin's wife was not well enough to attend, but Asia, accompanied by one of her daughters and Edwina, occupied a box overlooking the stage.

At the opening, Booth played the title role and Irving the villainous Iago. Both actors received ovations on their entrances and even louder applause at the final curtain. They traded roles at the end of the week, and Booth received even better reviews as Iago than he had as Othello. The critic for *Macmillan's Magazine* praised him for his subtlety. "He leans against the sundial, alert to execute any command of his master [Othello], seemingly careless what goes on so long as he is ready when wanted, yet ever watching his prey with sly, sleepless vigilance."

As the sold-out run of *Othello* continued, Booth wrote William Winter, "Only my domestic misery prevents it from being the happiest theatrical experience I've ever had." His wife's parents had arrived in London a short time before, and their daughter began at once to fill them with her wild imaginings. She told them that Edwin no longer loved her and had set out deliberately to ruin her life. Unfortunately for Booth, the McVickers believed her.

Edwin Booth as Iago in Shakespeare's *Othello*. *The Library of Congress.*

One of the last photographs of
the Booth family—Edwin,
Edwina, and the unfortunate
Mary McVicker.
*The Harvard Theatre Collection,
Houghton Library*

On June 16, Booth acted with Irving in *Othello* for the last time, and just
two days later he and his wife, her parents, and Edwina sailed for New York
from the port of Liverpool. Originally Edwin had planned to tour the
English provinces on his own following his engagement with Irving. But
the McVickers, whom Edwin privately called the "McWickeds," wanted to
get their daughter home to America, and Booth felt he must go with them.
Otherwise, the pair might accuse him of deserting his ailing wife.

Relations between Booth and his in-laws did not improve after the
party's arrival in New York. Booth rented a suite of rooms at the Windsor
Hotel for himself, his wife, and Edwina, but Mary Booth barely tolerated
her husband's presence. When he entered her room, she was more likely
than not to erupt in a convulsion of rage.

In the meantime, friends of the McVickers, or perhaps the McVickers
themselves, leaked stories to the city's more sensational newspapers accus-
ing Booth of "monstrous cruelty" to his wife. On the advice of his lawyer,

Booth did not respond to the charges, but he revealed his inmost feelings in a letter to his friend Winter. "All is now at sixes and sevens," Booth began. "On all sides I hear nothing but McVickers slanders—were it not for Mary's weakened condition and the scandal that would arise, I'd prosecute the she-devil [Mary's mother] for defamation of character and apply for a divorce from her lunatic daughter. I have sacrificed everything for this poor creature's whims and— but enough of this." A little later he ended the letter with a short, poignant sentence: "I'm tired out."

Adding to Booth's fatigue and distress that summer was the attempt on the life of President James A. Garfield by a frustrated office seeker, Charles J. Guiteau. As President Garfield fought for life—he lingered on until September 19—the newspapers published a wave of articles comparing Guiteau's act with John Wilkes Booth's deadly deed. "Will that horrible business never be buried?" Edwin wrote Asia. In an attempt to put forth his own position once and for all, he decided to reply to a letter from the historian Nahum Capen requesting information about John. As far as is known, this is Edwin's only written impression of his brother.

Windsor Hotel, N.Y.
July 28, 1881

To Nahum Capen
Dear Sir:

I can give you very little information regarding my brother John. I seldom saw him since his early boyhood in Baltimore. . . . We [his family] regarded him as a good-hearted, harmless, though wild-brained boy, and used to laugh at his patriotic faith whenever secession [of the South] was discussed. That he was insane on that one point, no one who knew him well can doubt. When I told him that I had voted for Lincoln's re-election, he expressed deep regret, and declared his belief that Lincoln would be made King of America; and this, I believe, drove him beyond the limits of reason. . . .

Knowing my sentiments, he avoided me, rarely visiting my house, except to see his mother, when political topics were not touched upon, at least in my presence. He was of a gentle, loving disposition, very boyish and full of fun—his mother's darling—and his deed and death crushed her spirit. He possessed rare dramatic talent and would have made a brilliant mark in the theatrical world. This is positively all that I know about him, having left him a mere schoolboy when I went with my father to California in 1852. On my return in '56 we were separated by professional engagements, which kept him mostly in the South, while I was employed in the Eastern and Northern states.

I do not believe any of the wild, romantic stories published in the papers concerning him; but of course he may have been engaged in political matters of which I knew nothing. All his theatrical friends speak of him as a poor, crazy boy, and such his family thought of him.

I am sorry I can afford you no further light on the subject.

Very truly yours,
Edwin Booth

Things soon came to a head in Booth's ongoing conflict with his wife and her parents. During the summer, Mary, backed by her mother, barred Booth from her room at the Windsor Hotel. In October, the McVickers moved Mary from the hotel to a house on West Fifty-third Street. That same month, Booth launched a four-week run in New York City, to be followed by a tour of the eastern states.

In late October, Booth wrote William Winter that his wife was willing to see him but only if he would admit he was a "villain" and write an apology and an acknowledgment of guilt to her parents. "People," Booth told Winter, "who have used me for their purposes and slandered me most vilely in return for all the slave-like devotion to their daughter these many years. On such conditions Mary will never see me in the flesh and I hope not in the Spirit—for God knows I've had enough of the McVicker tribe."

He went on to refer indirectly to his one-time dependence on alcohol: "You may judge how near madness I've been at times myself; passing sleepless nights after heavy work and not daring to stimulate [take a drink] for fear of falling off my perch, which but a pint of mild beer can accomplish for me."

Despite Edwin's disgust with the McVickers, he paid all of Mary's bills as soon as they were presented to him. But this did not go on for long. On November 13, while Booth was acting in Philadelphia, he received a brief telegram backstage: "Mrs. Booth died at five o'clock." Edwin interrupted his tour to attend Mary's funeral in New York with Edwina and several friends. Then he and William Winter took the train to Chicago, where Mary was buried in the McVicker family plot on November 18. Later, in a note to Winter thanking him for his support, Booth wrote: "God knows I'd rather no more should be said of poor Mary's mistakes. I want to forget all that was wrong and remember only the right—the true and good of the poor girl."

Chapter 20
TRIUMPH IN GERMANY

AFTER HIS WIFE'S DEATH, Edwina accompanied Edwin on his theatrical tours. Booth wrote his friend William Winter, "She enjoys the travel very much—that is the variety part of it, not the bumps and thumps we get [from the train tracks]."

The Booths traveled in luxury, according to the standards of the day. They rode in a private, hotel-style railroad car, with a sleeping compartment for each of them and a shared parlor complete with easy chairs, bookcases, and a piano. The rest of the acting company rode in an adjoining Pullman car whose seats could be converted into berths at night. Edwin often invited his fellow actors to join him and his daughter in their car for lunch. Afterward, Edwina would play popular tunes on the piano, and many of the guests would break into song.

Besides the pleasure she took from traveling with her father, Edwina had something else to be excited about in that winter of 1881–82. The previous autumn she had met and fallen in love with Downing Vaux, the charming but moody son of Calvert Vaux, codesigner of New York's Central Park. The young couple became engaged, and they planned to be married in the fall of 1883. First, though, Edwina would accompany her father on an extensive foreign tour that would take him to England, Ireland, Germany, and Austria.

The Booths set sail for England on June 14, 1882. Traveling with them as a youthful companion for Edwina was Downing Vaux's sister, Julia. In London, Booth received even more enthusiastic reviews from the critics than he had gotten the year before. He followed up his London success with a tour of British provincial cities, then crossed the Irish Sea to Dublin, where his acting was highly praised by the Irish critics. One wrote: "There would seem to be almost universal recognition amongst the Dublin public that Mr. Booth is a great actor."

Edwin, his daughter, and Julia Vaux spent Christmas 1882 in London, and Edwina was delighted when her fiancé, Downing Vaux, arrived by ship on December 22 to join the party. The holiday was less than festive, however. "The gloom and dampness of the English winter depress me very much," Edwin wrote to a friend. The weather had an especially damaging effect on Downing, making him nervous and short-tempered.

On December 27, the Booths and the two Vauxs were glad to leave London for Berlin, where Edwin was to begin a five-city tour of Germany and Austria. The tour presented Booth with a huge challenge: He would be acting his roles in English while the rest of the cast played their parts in German. As opening night approached, Booth grew more and more apprehensive. Would the evening turn out to be an interesting experiment or a hopeless mess?

For his first appearance in Berlin, Edwin chose to play Hamlet. The production got off to an uneasy start, with Edwin having to mentally translate each line of dialogue his fellow actors spoke to him in German, then respond with the appropriate words in his native English. It required tremendous concentration, but he made only one serious blunder, when he mistook a pause for his cue in the graveyard scene and plunged into his next speech before his partner had finished.

Few people in the audience seemed to notice, however. And when the final curtain fell and Edwin stepped forward to take his bow, he received an ovation the like of which he had rarely experienced. Waves of applause were topped with shouts of "Bravo!" in what seemed like an unending crescendo. The audience called Booth back onstage for no less than twenty-four bows before it finally let him go.

The reviews in the Berlin newspapers the next morning were just as ecstatic. "Booth is the best Hamlet I have ever seen," wrote the critic of the *Tagliche Berliner Rundschau.* "You can understand him perfectly even though you may not know a single word of what he utters."

The *Berliner Fremdenblatt* found fresh superlatives to describe his performance. "Booth's Hamlet is a masterpiece of the actor's genius . . . towering above all his rivals. . . . The curtain fell upon the most wonderful impersonation of Hamlet that Berlin has ever seen. . . . This Hamlet was not played, but lived."

Booth responded modestly to his Berlin triumph, but Edwina could not restrain her pride in her father. She wrote William Winter: "If you could but witness Papa's various performances, I am sure you would marvel at their continued vigor, and at the remarkable smoothness and ease with which he follows his fellow-actors."

She went on to tell Winter about the adulation Booth received following his last performance in Berlin. "It was a fitting close to his preceding triumphs, being the occasion for flattering presentations from the German actors and the public. . . . The actors gave him a beautiful wreath of silver, and there were many wreaths of genuine bay leaves from the public. The members of the company bade him quite a touching farewell, many of them embracing him! In the street his carriage was surrounded by enthusiastic men and women, waving their hats and handkerchiefs—some calling out *'Auf Wiedersehen!'* The same scene was repeated on our departure from the railway station."

What Edwina didn't describe to Winter was the sad turn her relationship with Downing Vaux had taken. The young man sank into an alarming depression in Germany. He showed no interest in his surroundings, or even in his fiancée. Booth took Vaux to see a German specialist in diseases of the nerves and brain, but the doctor was unable to help him. At last, it was decided that the best thing would be for Vaux to return to America with his sister, and the two of them set sail for New York in late February.

Edwina was naturally distressed by Vaux's illness and departure, and Booth couldn't help but be affected also. To see Edwina so downhearted took the edge off his success, "or rather my enjoyment of it," as he wrote a friend. "She is lonely and depressed of course—having no companion but old fogy me."

Both father and daughter carried on, however, and the reception Edwin got in the other German cities he visited almost equaled his triumph in Berlin. He was given a silver sprig of laurel in Hamburg, a silver crown of laurel in Bremen, and a silver wreath of laurel in Leipzig. (The ancient Greeks crowned the winners of various contests with wreaths woven from the leaves of laurel trees, and such wreaths have been associated with victors ever since.) The adoration heaped on him by the German critics and

Edwin Booth and his daughter, Edwina, in a photograph
taken during Booth's tour of Germany and Austria.
Shaw Collection, The Harvard Theatre Collection, Houghton Library

theatergoers "stimulates me strangely," Booth confessed to William Winter. "I feel more like acting than I have felt for years."

The only shadows on his success were the biographical articles that appeared in the German newspapers prior to his first performance in each of the cities on his tour. Almost all the articles emphasized his connection to John Wilkes and found space to recount yet again the story of Lincoln's assassination. Booth sent some of the articles to William Winter "to show you how even here I am compelled to taste the bitter dregs of my past. . . ." There was one small blessing, however. Since the articles were in German, he couldn't read them for himself.

The last stop on Booth's tour was Vienna, Austria, where he was hailed for his interpretation of the title role in *King Lear*. On his last night in Vienna, his fellow actors gave him the most beautiful of all the laurel wreaths he had received. Its leaves were of alternating gold and silver, and on each of them was engraved the name of a member of the company.

The Viennese urged Booth to stay longer in their city, and his German managers pleaded with him to return to Germany for an extended tour. Other acting offers came to him from France, Italy, Spain, and Russia. But Booth refused them all and prepared to return home with Edwina. "Well, 'tis over," he wrote to William Winter. "The experiment proved successful and I've no doubt—if I had a year to delve a little deeper here—I could do some good and lasting work. . . . But I am thoroughly tired and yearn for rest."

The Booths sailed for New York on June 1, 1883. Soon after their arrival, they learned that, far from getting better, Downing Vaux had steadily declined since his return home. There was no name for his condition then, but today doctors would probably say he had suffered a nervous breakdown. In any case, he was obviously in no shape to get married, and Edwina had no choice but to break off their engagement.

To ease his daughter's disappointment and sorrow, Edwin bought a summer house on the rocky Rhode Island shore not far from Newport. He christened the place Boothden, and he and Edwina spent the summer there, lazing on the porch or cruising on Booth's small yacht. That fall, before going on tour, Booth bought a winter home for himself and his daughter in Boston, a city he had always loved. It was a gray stone mansion on exclusive Beacon Hill, with a wrought-iron fence in front and purple glass in the drawing-room windows.

Edwina enjoyed playing hostess and housekeeper for her "dear Papa" when he was home in Boston or at Boothden. But then, in the fall of 1884, she met Ignatius Grossman, a Hungarian immigrant who had built a successful career as a stockbroker in Boston. After a whirlwind romance, Edwina and Grossman became engaged, and their wedding was set for May 1885. Edwin admitted to William Winter that he dreaded losing his daughter. "And yet I am sure that the man she has chosen will be a tender, devoted husband," Booth wrote of Grossman. "His record is of the purest, and all who know him endorse him in the highest terms."

The marriage of Edwina and Ignatius Grossman took place in her father's Beacon Hill home, and afterward the newlyweds left on a honeymoon trip to England. Edwin saw their ship off in New York, then returned alone to the house in Boston. Sitting in his den eight days later, he wrote to Edwina in England. "My darling, I can't tell you just how I feel—the separation has been a wrench to my nerves; but when in the midst of my selfishness the thought comes of your happiness and the good that will come to you, I cease to grieve."

Edwina's leaving home was not the only loss Booth suffered in the mid-1880s. His older brother, June, had died in Manchester, New Hampshire, in September 1883, soon after Edwin's return from Germany. June had left the theater some years earlier and had gone into the hotel business. He was managing a seaside hotel in Manchester at the time of his death. Edwin and his surviving brother, Joseph, attended June's funeral, but their mother—now in her eighties and ailing—was too frail to travel to New Hampshire.

Then, in October 1885, Edwin received the sad news that his mother, too, was gone. She had passed away in her sleep in her New York home at the age of eighty-four, attended by her devoted daughter Rosalie. When Booth arrived in New York later that day and turned back the sheet that covered his mother's face, he was amazed at how calm and youthful she looked. The last time he had seen her alive, she had seemed to be weighed down by her long years of suffering. "The end was a blessing," Booth wrote to a friend, "and to all who loved her a sense of relief has buoyed rather than depressed us."

Edwin Booth in the 1880s. *The Harvard Theatre Collection, Houghton Library*

Edwin, Joseph, and Rosalie accompanied their mother's body to Baltimore, where she was buried beside their father in Greenmount Cemetery. The graveside service took place an hour earlier than the time listed in the Baltimore newspapers. That way the family avoided any curiosity seekers who might have been drawn to the ceremony, hoping to see Mrs. Booth laid to rest near her son John.

In the spring of 1886, Booth had several warnings of his own mortality. He was only fifty-two, but years of touring and sleepless nights, coupled with heavy smoking (sometimes a pipe but more often cigars), had taken their toll on his health. In February 1886, near the end of a demanding tour, he went on one night as Brutus in Shakespeare's *Julius Caesar*, a role he had played hundreds of times, and suddenly couldn't remember his lines. Eventually he got back on track, but not before "making a bungle of the part," as he put it in a letter to William Winter.

Something even more embarrassing happened two months later, when he was in New York costarring in a series of plays with the renowned Italian actor Tommaso Salvini. Ever since his last tour of England, Booth had been bothered by occasional spells of dizziness that made him stumble or fall. His doctors diagnosed this lightheadedness as vertigo and blamed it on his smoking. They urged him to stop or at least cut back. Booth tried, but found it difficult if not impossible to alter such a long-standing habit. Fortunately, the dizziness didn't affect his acting—not, that is, until the night of April 28, 1886, when Booth was playing Iago to Tommaso Salvini's Othello in a performance of Shakespeare's tragedy.

In one scene, a suspicious Othello hurls Iago to the floor in anger, then yanks him back to his feet. But when Salvini pulled Booth to his feet, Edwin felt dizzy and fell backward, breaking through the rail between the stage and the footlights and putting out three of the gas jets. He might have dropped down into the orchestra pit if a fast-acting musician hadn't shoved him back onto the stage.

The audience sat in stunned silence as Salvini helped Edwin to his feet once more. Booth managed to gather his forces and carry on with the play, but in the last act he was overcome by another wave of dizziness. He sank onto a chair, his head lolled to one side, and his legs stretched out straight in front of him. Sensing his plight, several small-part players stood between Booth and the audience until the actor had a chance to pull himself together.

Many in the theater that night—and many journalists who wrote about the performance the next day—were convinced that Booth was drunk. "History repeats itself!" read one headline. "Never was Edwin Booth seen to worse advantage," trumpeted another article. Booth himself protested that drink had nothing to do with his behavior. He had rehearsed all day, he said, and was exhausted. His doctor had urged him not to perform that night, but he had insisted on being driven to the theater. He decided not to say anything about the attacks of vertigo, fearing disclosure might make managers reluctant to hire him in the future.

Gradually the gossip and speculation died down, but in the meantime Booth continued to suffer. "My misery is not yet ended," he wrote to a friend in early May. "Every day some ugly reference to my misfortune appears and I am heartsick."

Fortunately, there were several developments in his life that helped to take his mind off his health problems. In March, Edwina had given birth to her first child, a daughter whom she and her husband named Mildred. Now Booth had a new role to play—that of a doting grandfather.

Professionally, he had recently received a major boost also. The well-known actor-manager Lawrence Barrett proposed that he and Booth join forces and go on a series of tours together. With their names on the marquee, the tours were sure to be successful, Barrett said. Not only would they make a good income for themselves, but the profits would enable them to hire an outstanding company to play the supporting parts.

What appealed most to Booth, however, was Barrett's promise that he would handle all the business arrangements for the tours. Ever since his own theater had failed, Booth had hated the haggling with managers that was involved in scheduling a season and making travel plans. With Barrett to take care of those things, Booth would be free to concentrate on his acting. Perhaps he would even be able to recapture the youthful energy and excitement he had felt in Germany.

Chapter 21
A Toast to the Players

My God, you look as if you had been scalped by Indians," Edwin Booth exclaimed.

That critical comment about her makeup was how Edwin introduced himself to Kitty Malony, one of the young players Lawrence Barrett had assembled for his first cross-country tour with Booth. Years later Malony wrote about her experiences during that tour in a book titled *Behind the Scenes with Edwin Booth.*

Up until the moment Booth criticized it, Kitty thought she was creating a suitably frightening look for the role she was playing that day. She had been cast as the Bloody Apparition, the ghost of one of the title character's many victims in Shakespeare's *Macbeth.* Now, looking in the mirror, she wasn't so sure.

"Should I take it off?" she asked Booth.

"I should hope so," the star replied. He reached for a towel and wiped off all the greasepaint and red coloring that Kitty had applied. Then he picked up her makeup brush and, after studying the contours of her face, painted on the stage blood himself—but much more lightly this time.

They looked at the result together, and Kitty had to admit it was more convincing. "There should be enough skin left exposed to prove it was a human being who was slaughtered," Booth said.

As the tour progressed, Booth took a special liking to Kitty and her young friends in the company, Emma Vaders and Ida Rock. They helped to fill the actor's need for companionship, which his daughter Edwina had provided on earlier tours. Booth often invited Kitty and her friends to dine with him in his private railroad car. Afterward, he would light up an after-dinner cigar and entertain the young women with stories about his early experiences traveling with his father and performing in the Gold Rush boomtowns of California.

Booth confided that he often suffered from insomnia. When the evening came to an end, he would thank Kitty and the others for helping to drive away "the vultures" that descended on him while he lay sleepless. "Memories are hard on one in the lonely hours," he added.

Kitty guessed that Booth was thinking, among other things, of his brother John and the terrible crime he had committed. But the actor never spoke of John in any of his conversations with Kitty.

When the tour reached its last stop in New Bedford, Massachusetts, in the spring of 1887, Kitty and her friends, and Booth, were all sorry to see it come to an end. Booth proclaimed it "the happiest season of his career." And Kitty found herself crying as she said goodbye to Booth. "I think I know why I cried," she wrote later. "I knew I would not see as fine a human being any time soon."

That summer Edwin decided to sell his house on Beacon Hill in Boston. He also put Boothden, his summer retreat in Rhode Island, on the market. With Edwina no longer available to keep him company, both places seemed too big for him. He didn't enjoy roaming from room to room with only himself to talk to.

The proceeds from the two houses added to Booth's already considerable wealth. Now that Lawrence Barrett was handling the financial arrangements for his tours, Booth was making more money from his acting than he ever had. His income from the 1886–87 tour alone was more than $200,000. That was a huge amount at a time when the average working-man made nine dollars a week, and the weekly salary of a skilled professional—a doctor or lawyer—might be fifteen or sixteen dollars.

Booth's problem was not earning more money but deciding how to spend what he had. He had always been generous with Edwina and the members of his family when any of them needed something. He was also known as a soft touch if an old actor or actress came to him pleading poverty. At any given time he contributed to the support of a dozen or more performers who had fallen on hard times. But now, as he got older and his bank balance grew larger, he longed to embark on a bigger project that would benefit even more people. He conceived the idea of a club for actors,

Edwin Booth with his business partner and costar
Lawrence Barrett (*left*). *Evert Jansen Wendell Collection,
The Harvard Theatre Collection, Houghton Library*

and was still working out the details when he took a yachting trip up the
Atlantic coast with friends in the summer of 1887.

The new club would be more than just a gathering place for theater people, Booth told his traveling companions. He had long felt that most
actors—including himself—were too limited in their outlook. Consequently, his club would be open to members from other professions. In the
relaxed atmosphere of the clubhouse, actors, doctors, writers, and businessmen would have the opportunity to meet and mingle, and each member's horizons would be broadened.

As the yachting party sailed north, Booth outlined more of his plans for the club. He would endow it with a suitable building in New York City, he said, and decorate the rooms with theatrical memorabilia from his own collection of portraits, playbills, costumes, and props. All he would expect for himself were several rooms on the premises in which he could set up an apartment.

He hadn't yet thought of a name for the club, Booth admitted. But a fellow passenger on the yacht, the writer Thomas Bailey Aldrich, came up with a suggestion that Edwin and the others aboard liked at once: the Players.

Even as he made plans for the future, Edwin found himself thrust back into the past. It happened when the yacht docked briefly at Boothbay Harbor, Maine. Edwin went shopping in a drugstore and casually asked the owner where the town had got its name. Not knowing to whom he was speaking, the druggist began his reply by saying the name had nothing to do with "that damned scoundrel who killed Lincoln."

A thin-lipped Edwin didn't give the owner a chance to finish his story. Instead, he laid the money for his purchase on the counter and strode out of the store. More than twenty years had passed since the assassination, but Booth could still be shaken by the slightest reminder of John's deed. He could not bear to look at a picture of Abraham Lincoln, and he refrained from any mention of his brother's name, even among his closest friends.

Plans for the Players moved forward swiftly in the next few months. Booth went on tour again with Lawrence Barrett in the fall of 1887, but he authorized a friend in New York to seek a home for the club. The man found a town house on fashionable Gramercy Park that he thought would be appropriate, and Booth agreed, although the price for the property— $150,000—was more than he had expected to pay.

Once the house had been acquired, Booth spared no expense in remodeling it to suit the club's needs. The noted architect Stanford White was engaged to carry out the renovations. These included a handsome series of meeting rooms and a members' dining room on the first floor, and on the third floor an apartment for Booth that looked down on Gramercy Park.

The actor had to interrupt his tour in the spring of 1888 when word came that his sister Asia Booth Clarke had died of heart disease in England. Her husband, John, brought her body home for burial, and Edwin accompanied his sister's coffin to Baltimore, where it was interred in the family plot at Greenmount Cemetery.

Neither John Clarke nor Edwin ever knew of a manuscript that Asia had been secretly writing for years and had completed shortly before her death. It was a memoir of her brother John, beginning with the carefree childhood days they had spent together and ending with John's final visit to her home a few weeks before the assassination. Fearing that her husband, who hated John, would destroy the manuscript if he knew of its existence, Asia had entrusted it to an English friend for safekeeping and possible publication after her death.

The renovation of the Players, Edwin's pride and joy, was finally finished in December 1888, and the grand opening of the club was set for New Year's Eve. Edwin presided over the celebration. Standing beneath a portrait of his father, Junius, in the first-floor parlor, he raised a silver cup of wine and said, "Let us drink from this loving cup, this souvenir of long ago, my father's flagon. Let us now, beneath his portrait, drink to the Players' perpetual prosperity." He raised the cup to his lips, took a small sip of wine, and passed the cup to the other founding members who were standing in a circle around him.

Edwina had sent the organizers of the celebration a present for her father, asking that it be given to him during the ceremony. The present was a laurel wreath like those that had been presented to Edwin in Germany, and a card from Edwina accompanied it. On the card, she had written simply "Hamlet, King [referring to King Lear], Father."

When the wreath was handed to Edwin and he read the words on the card, emotion gripped him. He tried to say something, stopped three times, cleared his throat, and finally whispered, "I think I can say no more." Soon afterward, he retired to his apartment on the third floor while the gala party continued downstairs.

The Players was an immediate success. Among its earliest members were the writer Mark Twain, the stage star George M. Cohan, and President Grover Cleveland. Not all the members were well known. Edwin realized that many younger theater people who would benefit most from exchanging ideas with established professionals could not afford to join the Players. To aid them, he arranged to pay the initiation fees and membership dues for fifty of the most promising young applicants each year.

Soon after the Players opened, Booth resumed touring under Lawrence Barrett's management. "Hard work seems to agree with me this season," he wrote to William Winter. "But I must confess travel and irregular meals do not." On April 3, 1889, he was scheduled to costar with Barrett in Shakespeare's *Othello* in Rochester, New York. Booth felt odd during the ride to the theater but thought it was just nerves.

The problem was more serious than that, however. When Booth arrived at the theater and tried to greet the old doorman, no words came out. Still, he got into Iago's costume, sure that when he walked onstage, his voice would return. It did not. Booth made every effort to deliver Iago's first lines, but all he could produce was gibberish.

Watching from the wings, a stunned Lawrence Barrett ordered the curtain to be lowered and sent a stagehand for a doctor. Then Barrett walked before the curtain and told the audience there would be no performance that night. Thinking that Booth had suffered a stroke, he went on, "We fear that this is the beginning of the end. The world may have heard for the last time the voice of the greatest actor who speaks the English language."

Picking up on Barrett's words, many newspapers ran stories the next day that proclaimed "Edwin Booth Is Dying." But Edwin had rallied overnight and, though still weak, had regained his voice. Even so, Barrett called a halt to the tour so that Booth could consult with his own doctors in New York. They said he had suffered an attack of "nervous prostration," not a stroke, and prescribed a week or ten days of "absolute rest." They also advised him once again to cut back drastically on his smoking.

By then Booth was feeling so much better that he ignored the doctors' advice and the urgings of his daughter, Edwina, and insisted on resuming the tour. He was back on the road by the middle of April and performing as well as ever. But he did acknowledge in a note to Barrett that "I have received my second warning [the first had been the attack of dizziness suffered while acting with Salvini], and we can't tell when I'll get the notice to quit." Booth also decided that Iago was an unlucky role for him; he had been playing it when he was felled by vertigo, and was about to perform the same part when he lost his voice.

Booth spent most of the summer of 1889 resting quietly in his apartment at the Players—what he called "my nest among the tree-tops of Gramercy Park." In August he traveled to Narragansett, Rhode Island, where Edwina

Edwin Booth relaxing with his grandchildren, Mildred and Edwin Grossman. *The Harvard Theatre Collection, Houghton Library*

and her family were vacationing. Edwin now had two grandchildren to dote on—four-year-old Mildred and her younger brother, Edwin, who had recently turned three. Visitors to the resort delighted in watching Booth read aloud to the children on the veranda and hearing his famous voice call out "Moo!" or "Bow-wow!"

That fall Booth went on the road again, this time opposite the famous Polish actress Helena Modjeska. Lawrence Barrett handled the business arrangements for the tour, as usual, but did not travel with the company. He had come down with a mysterious disease of the glands and was undergoing treatment for it at a spa in Germany. Fortunately, Edwin's health held up throughout the season, although he often felt tired. "The vigor that I occasionally manifest is nervous force merely," he wrote to William Winter, "and, like a stimulant, leaves me in a collapsed condition."

Painting of Edwin Booth late in his career, in costume for the title role in the play *Richelieu*. *The Library of Congress*

While performing in Chicago in the spring of 1890, Booth recorded several speeches from Shakespeare's plays for Thomas Edison's new invention, the phonograph. He planned to give the recording to Edwina's children so that, in later years, they could hear what their grandfather sounded like. Today, Booth's recordings are included on discs of actors from the past that can be found in the theater collections of many libraries. His simple, direct interpretations contrast sharply with the flamboyant style employed by many of his contemporaries. When you listen to the recordings, it's easy to see why Booth stood out as unique in his own time. It's also apparent how great an influence his more natural approach had on the actors who followed him, down to the present.

Lawrence Barrett rejoined Booth and the rest of the company in the fall of 1890. But Barrett's glandular condition was no better; if anything, it had gotten worse. His throat hurt constantly, his voice was muffled, and his face was badly swollen. Still, he insisted on playing all his usual roles, and he and Edwin continued to draw crowds, largely on the basis of their past reputations.

The newspaper reviewers were not as tolerant as the fans. "Nowhere but at a public funeral and a public performance of Shakespeare do we parade the relics of departed worth," wrote the drama critic of the *New York World* when Booth and Barrett opened their New York season in March 1891. The critic's harshest comments were reserved for Edwin. He described him as "the tottering Mr. Booth . . . whose work was marked and marred by a careless feebleness."

Edwina was furious with the *World* review and expressed her outrage in a letter to her father. In his reply, Edwin did his best to assure her that he had taken the review in stride. "'Tis childish to be crushed by such vile wretches, with whom no reputation is sacred," he wrote. "The public man (or woman) must bear the scorn, and stand unshaken by it, as I have done."

Perhaps Booth was thinking of other times, and more serious personal crises, like the six months following the assassination when he wondered if he would ever act again. In any case, despite advancing age and his various ailments, he now seemed determined to forge ahead.

Chapter 22
THE LAST *HAMLET*

*E*DWIN FELT MORE ENERGETIC than usual on the evening of March 18, 1891, and was giving one of his better recent performances in the title role of *Richelieu*. Until the middle of the third act, at least. That was when his costar, Lawrence Barrett, bent over the bed on which Booth as Cardinal Richelieu was lying and broke out of character to whisper, "I can't go on."

Barrett's glandular condition had flared up earlier while he was applying his makeup, and Edwin had tried to persuade him not to perform that night. Barrett had insisted, however, and seemed to be in control of the situation until he told Booth he could not continue. Barrett managed to finish the scene and make his exit, but his understudy had to replace him for the rest of the play.

Back at his hotel, Barrett was put to bed with a severe cold and high fever, and his understudy filled in for him the next two nights. Edwin was concerned for his costar and friend but not really alarmed; Barrett had surmounted his health problems thus far, and Booth was confident he would do so again. This time was different, though. Weakened by his glandular infection, Barrett was unable to fight off the cold, which soon developed into pneumonia. In less than three days the actor-manager was dead.

Edwin was desolate. He had come to rely on Barrett to handle all the business details connected with his theatrical career, and he could not imagine going on without him. For the sake of the other actors in the company, Booth finished out the last weeks of the Manhattan engagement, playing opposite Barrett's understudy. He found it hard to rise above his depression, however, and the critics were quick to take note of it. "Mr. Booth has gone wearily and wearisomely through the final weeks of his season here," one wrote, "delivering the blank verse of Shakespeare blankly indeed, and presenting so weak a sight as to be pitiful."

Barrett had booked the company for a week at the Brooklyn Academy of Music following the end of the Manhattan run, and Edwin was determined to honor the commitment. The last play on the Brooklyn schedule was a matinee performance of *Hamlet* on April 4 with Edwin, as usual, in the title role.

No one had announced that it would be Booth's final appearance that spring, let alone that it would mark the end of his acting career. It's doubtful if Edwin himself had made any firm decisions about his future at this point. Yet the overflow crowd that clamored for tickets outside the Academy of Music behaved as if it would be their last chance to see the fabled actor onstage.

If they had expected an outstanding production, they were disappointed. The supporting cast gave routine performances without Barrett to keep them in line, and the prop man forgot to put any earth in the pit for the gravediggers' scene. Edwin started off weakly also. His gray hair made it difficult to believe he was a brooding young prince, and he pitched his voice so low that those in the back rows had a hard time hearing him. Booth rose to the occasion, however, in his confrontations with Ophelia, and his voice gained strength as the performance went on. There were more than a few moments when his genius as an actor was still apparent. One of them came during the famed "To be, or not to be" soliloquy. A Broadway producer who was present, David Belasco, said, "The familiar words seemed to come from Booth's lips for the first time."

At the end, the audience rose as one to its feet and erupted in an outburst of applause, shouts, and cheers. Booth appeared to be genuinely moved as he walked forward to acknowledge this tremendous display of affection. And although he rarely did so, he made a brief speech. "Ladies and gentlemen, I thank you for your great kindness," he began. "I hope this is not the last time I shall have the honor of appearing before you. . . . I hope that my health and strength may be improved so that I can serve you better, and I shall always try to deserve the favor you have shown me."

Booth bowed low at the end, and then stepped back as the curtains closed for the last time. He removed his costume and scrubbed off his makeup quickly, as he always did, and was one of the first actors to leave

Edwin Booth in 1892. This was one of the last photographs of the actor.
The Harvard Theatre Collection, Houghton Library

the theater. Outside in the street, a huge crowd surrounded him while he walked to his carriage. They seemed reluctant to let Booth go as he climbed aboard, and policemen cleared a path for the vehicle to proceed on its trip to New York City. The carriage moved forward slowly through the crowd, and Booth turned first to one side and then the other, tipping his hat as he did so. Some in the front of the throng thought they saw tears in his eyes.

Edwin might have believed, on that afternoon in Brooklyn, that he would return to the stage one day, but he never did. He spent most of the next two years at the Players and expressed no regret that his days as a traveling player were over. "What I want now," he told William Winter, "is to stay in one place with things I like around me. . . . Here is my bed, and here is the fire, and here are my books, and here you come to see me. I suppose I shall wear out here."

His health was not good. Long years of smoking had taken their toll, weakening his heart and making him short of breath. When he took a stroll around Gramercy Park, he had to lean on a friend's arm. His life brightened after Edwina and her family moved from Boston to New York and took an apartment not far from the Players. It was good to have Edwina close at hand again, and he always enjoyed a visit from his grandchildren, even when they tired him out with their demands that he read them a story.

Booth's life went forward in this quiet fashion until April 17, 1893, when he suffered a stroke that paralyzed his right arm and side. In the weeks that followed, he regained some of his mobility, but his speech remained thick and hard to understand. Edwina and her husband only hoped he would be strong enough to spend the summer with them on the Rhode Island shore. Then, on June 3rd, he had a relapse. A bulletin posted downstairs at the Players informed members of his condition: "Mr. Booth has gradually grown weaker during the past twenty-four hours, and there is now very little hope left of even a partial recovery."

Edwina brought her children to say goodbye to their grandfather. "How are you, dear Grandpa?" little Edwin asked.

Booth, who had been dozing, roused himself and fixed his gaze on his grandson. "How are you yourself, old fellow?" he replied with a smile. According to Edwina, those were the last words her father ever spoke.

By June 6, it was obvious the end was near. Edwina sat patiently by Booth's bed as the hours passed. A severe thunderstorm hit the city just before midnight on the sixth, and lightning flashed through Booth's room. Then, around one in the morning of June 7, the lights suddenly went out. When they came on again a few moments later, Edwina turned to her father and realized that he had died.

Booth's funeral was held on June 9, 1893, at the Little Church Around the Corner, a favorite of actors. It is located on East 29th Street, just nine blocks north of the Players. One hundred fifty members of the club, all on foot, accompanied the hearse to the church. After the service, Booth's coffin was taken to Grand Central Terminal for shipment by train to Boston. There, according to his wishes, he would be buried in Mount Auburn Cemetery beside his beloved first wife, Mary Devlin.

Edwin Booth's burial plot in Mount Auburn Cemetery in Cambridge, Massachusetts. Here his remains lie with those of his first wife, Mary Devlin, and his only son, Edgar, who lived less than a day.
The Harvard Theatre Collection, Houghton Library

Something strange happened as the train carrying Booth's body headed north. Ford's Theatre in Washington, the site of Lincoln's assassination, had been converted into an office building for use by the Records and Pensions Division of the War Department. That afternoon, without warning, three floors of the structure collapsed in an ear-splitting roar, killing more than twenty clerks and injuring twice that many.

Many newspapers the next morning contained accounts of both Edwin's funeral and the collapse of the former Ford's Theatre, noting the eerie coincidence between the two events. Even in death, it seemed, Edwin could not escape the shadow of his brother John's deadly act.

Today the Players endures in the home Edwin bought for the club on Gramercy Park, and so does Booth's reputation as the finest classical actor of his time. Moreover, theater people have not only gained the respect Booth sought for them, but the study of theater is now a recognized part of the curriculum in many of America's leading colleges and universities. Unlike Booth, who always felt his own lack of a formal education, students today can obtain advanced degrees in acting, directing, playwriting, set design, and other dramatic arts.

But for every person who knows that there was once a great actor named Edwin Booth, there are thousands who know that his brother, John Wilkes Booth, assassinated Abraham Lincoln. This is yet another example of the long-held truism that villains in fiction and in life are more interesting and colorful than heroes. Besides, John wasn't just any villain. He was the first in a long line of men and women who, for various reasons, killed or tried to kill a president of the United States. And his target was Abraham Lincoln, who would become arguably America's most beloved president. No wonder John Wilkes Booth is still talked about, and still detested, today.

Real life is more complicated than fiction, however. Edwin Booth, especially in his hard-drinking younger years, did not always fit the stereotype of the "good brother." Nor did John, as a young actor and bon vivant, deserve the label "bad brother." Reckless and rambunctious, yes, but not necessarily evil. All of that was forgotten, though, in light of John's final, murderous act—the act that ensured he would be remembered only as the killer of Lincoln.

Except by those who knew him best, the members of his family. His mother could never forget the loving son John had been before the assassination. Asia, in her memoir, attempted to portray what she saw as her brother's better nature before it was overwhelmed by his irrational hatred of President Lincoln.

Even Edwin, who had every reason to despise his brother for bringing such pain and suffering to the nation and to Edwin himself, could not erase John from his memory. He might refuse to mention John's name in conversation, he might burn a trunk filled with his costumes and other possessions. But on display in Edwin's room at the Players when he died, along with photographs of his father and his first wife, was a photo of John Wilkes Booth as a young actor. John, the brother Edwin had loved in spite of everything.

BIBLIOGRAPHY AND SOURCE NOTES

*R*EADERS OFTEN WONDER where the author got the idea for the book. In the case of *Good Brother, Bad Brother,* the idea came to me one morning in the shower, complete with title. But it had its roots in almost a lifetime of personal interests and experience.

From teenage on, I've had a serious interest in the theater. I acted in numerous plays in high school, college, and summer stock, and eventually branched out into directing and playwriting. After I put my theatrical ambitions aside in favor of a career in children's books, I continued to attend the theater frequently and often thought it would be fun to write a book for young people about some aspect of the drama.

At the same time, I've had a longstanding fascination with the American Civil War—the monumental struggle that brought an end to slavery in the United States, but only after a horrendous loss of life on both sides of the conflict. I longed to write about it, too, but couldn't think of a focus.

Then came that fateful morning in the shower when my two interests suddenly merged. The result was this joint biography of the Booth brothers, played out against the backdrop of the Civil War.

A wide range of sources contributed to the research for the book. Three adult biographies—one of Edwin Booth, the other two of the Booth family—provided useful overviews of the material.

Prince of Players: Edwin Booth by Eleanor Ruggles (New York: W. W. Norton & Company, 1953) is a comprehensive, if sometimes rambling, account of the actor's life and includes an excellent bibliography. A bestseller in its day, it was made into a 1955 movie, now available on DVD, that starred the British actor Richard Burton as Edwin Booth.

The Mad Booths of Maryland by Stanley Kimmel (New York: Bobbs-Merrill Company, Inc., 1940; second revised and enlarged edition, New York: Dover Publications, Inc., 1969) is often as melodramatic in tone as its title but contains much illuminating information about the early life of Junius Brutus Booth, and on Edwin Booth's experiences in Gold Rush California and his travels to Australia and Hawaii.

American Gothic: The Story of America's Legendary Theatrical Family—Junius, Edwin, and John Wilkes Booth by Gene Smith (New York: Simon & Schuster, 1992) complements the Kimmel biography and is especially good on Edwin Booth's life after the assassination, the building of his theater, his second marriage, and the founding of the Players.

An abundance of primary source material is available on various members of the Booth family. In my research, I drew heavily on the following four titles:

Between Actor and Critic: Selected Letters of Edwin Booth and William Winter, edited with an introduction and commentary by David J. Watermeier (Princeton, New Jersey: Princeton University Press, 1971), is a compilation of letters Booth wrote to Winter, one of the foremost drama critics of his day, between February 1869, when Booth was thirty-five, and December 1890, two and a half years before the actor's death. Since Booth never kept a journal or wrote his autobiography, these letters provide one of the best records we have of his activities and shifting moods. The actor wrote most of the letters late at night, when he was winding down from the evening's performance.

Another book featuring Edwin Booth's letters offers intimate glimpses of the actor as a father. It is *Edwin Booth: Recollections by His Daughter Edwina Booth Grossman and Letters to Her and to His Friends* by Edwina Booth Grossman (New York: The Century Company, 1894; New York/London: Benjamin Blom, 1969). Particularly revealing are the letters, filled with kindly advice, that Booth wrote to his daughter when she was a child and a young adult.

Right or Wrong, God Judge Me: The Writings of John Wilkes Booth, edited by John Rhodehamel and Louise Taper (Urbana and Chicago: University of Illinois Press, 1997; first paperback edition, 2001), is a comprehensive gathering of the surviving correspondence and speeches of Lincoln's assassin, prefaced with excellent notes by the editors.

John Wilkes Booth: A Sister's Memoir by Asia Booth Clarke, edited and with an introduction by Terry Alford (Jackson, Mississippi: University Press of Mississippi, 1996; paperback edition, 1999), is an insightful portrait of Booth by one of the people who knew him best. It was originally published under the title *The Unlocked Book: A Memoir of John Wilkes Booth by His Sister, Asia Booth Clarke,* edited and with a foreword by Eleanor Farjeon (New York: G. P. Putnam's Sons, 1938). There's an interesting story behind the book's first publication. Asia Clarke wrote most of the manuscript in 1874, nine years after Lincoln's assassination and six years after she moved to England. She made additions and corrections to the text over the years, all the while keeping its existence a secret from her husband for fear he might destroy it. Shortly before her death, she entrusted the manuscript to an English friend, the novelist B. L. Farjeon, with instructions that he "publish it sometime" if he saw fit. It was Farjeon's daughter Eleanor, a well-known writer of stories and poems for children, who brought the memoir to the attention of her American publisher, G. P. Putnam's, and arranged for it to be published in 1938, fifty years after Asia's death.

A book that helped me to get a clearer picture of John Wilkes Booth as an actor was *Lust for Fame: The Stage Career of John Wilkes Booth* by Gordon Samples (Jefferson, North Carolina, and London: McFarland & Company, Inc., Publishers, 1982; first paperback edition, 1998). Samples fleshes out his account of Booth's theatrical career with many vivid anecdotes related by his fellow players, and includes at the back an exhaustive year-by-year list of the cities and towns where Booth appeared, the plays in which he performed, and the parts he played.

Other titles provided information for particular sections in the Booth brothers' story. These include:

Never Call Retreat by Bruce Catton (New York: Doubleday & Company, 1965; first paperback edition, New York: Washington Square Press, Pocket Books, Inc., 1967). A clear account of the last years of the Civil War and the death of Lincoln.

The Lincoln Murder Conspiracies by William Hanchett (Urbana and Chicago: University of Illinois Press, 1983). Includes thorough coverage of John Wilkes Booth's plots to kidnap Lincoln.

Our American Cousin: The Play That Changed History by Tom Taylor, edited and introduced by Welford Dunaway Taylor (Washington: Beacham Publishing, Inc., 1990). The complete text, with notes, of the play Lincoln went to see the night he was killed.

A. Lincoln: His Last 24 Hours by W. Emerson Reck (Jefferson, North Carolina: McFarland & Company, Inc., Publishers, 1987; first paperback edition, Columbia, South Carolina: The University of South Carolina Press, 1994). An hour-by-hour chronicle, filled with little-known facts.

April 1865: The Month That Saved America by Jay Winik (New York: HarperCollins Publishers, 2001). Includes a detailed description of the route Lincoln's funeral train followed on its way back to his native Illinois.

The Escape and Capture of John Wilkes Booth by Edward Steers, Jr. (Gettysburg, Pennsylvania: Thomas Publications, 1983, 1992). A vivid, step-by-step narrative.

Lincoln's Assassins: Their Trial and Execution: An Illustrated History by James L. Swanson and Daniel R. Weinberg (Santa Fe, New Mexico: Arena Editions, 2001). The text relies on well-chosen primary sources; the illustrations include engravings and political cartoons from magazines and newspapers of the period, as well as Alexander Gardner's revealing photographs of the accused.

Beyond the books I read, I benefited greatly from a tour of Ford's Theatre in Washington, now restored to its original state and host once more to a full schedule of plays and musicals. I sat in the orchestra amid a crowd of visiting young people and their parents and teachers—it was spring break. We looked up at the state box where President Lincoln sat on the fateful night of April 14, 1865, and heard the youthful guide describe John Wilkes Booth as "the Brad Pitt of his day." Afterward, a National Parks Service employee told me that the Ford's Theatre tour is the third most popular in Washington, after the White House and the F.B.I.

SOURCE NOTES BY CHAPTER

CHAPTER 1 End of the Civil War: Catton. Edwin's reaction to the news that John has shot Lincoln: Smith, as excerpted from *Crowding Memories* by Mrs. Thomas Bailey Aldrich (Lilian Woodman) (Boston: Houghton Mifflin Company, 1920). Letter to Edwin from the Boston Theatre's manager and Edwin's reply: Smith, as excerpted from *John Wilkes Booth: Fact and Fiction of Lincoln's Assassination* by Francis Wilson (Boston: Houghton Mifflin Company, 1929). Edwin's letter to Adam Badeau: Ruggles.

CHAPTER 2 Edwin's birth and early childhood: Ruggles. Junius Brutus Booth's background, his beginnings in the theater, and his meeting Mary Ann Holmes: Kimmel. Junius Booth's other family, his divorce from his first wife, Adelaide, and his belated marriage to Mary Ann: Kimmel, Ruggles.

CHAPTER 3 Edwin's life on the road with his father, and how he kept his father from straying: Ruggles. Edwin's dialogue with his father before his first appearance as an actor: Ruggles, as excerpted from *The Life and Art of Edwin Booth* by William Winter (New York: The Macmillan Company, 1893). The night Edwin substituted for his father in the role of Richard III: Ruggles, as excerpted from Winter. Junius and Edwin's departure for California: Ruggles, Kimmel.

CHAPTER 4 The Booths' journey to California and Edwin's first impressions of San Francisco: Kimmel, Ruggles. Junius's recommendation that Edwin play Hamlet: Kimmel. June's advice to Edwin to put a slug in the bottom of his trunk: Ruggles. Edwin's experiences in the gold-mining towns: Kimmel. The younger Booth's reaction when he hears that his father has died: Kimmel, Ruggles. Junius Booth's last days and his death: Kimmel, Ruggles.

CHAPTER 5 Edwin's first appearance in the role of Hamlet and two reviewers' impressions of his performance: Kimmel. Background of actress Laura Keene: Ruggles, Kimmel, *Columbia Encyclopedia*. Edwin's quip about Keene: Ruggles. Voyage to Australia, and Edwin's experiences there: Kimmel, Ruggles. *Richard III* and *Hamlet* in Honolulu: Kimmel, Ruggles. Edwin's return to California and his erratic behavior: Kimmel. June's impressions of the teenage John Wilkes: Kimmel. Edwin's decision to go home to Maryland, and his preparations for the trip: Kimmel. The developing conflict over slavery in the new Midwestern states: *Columbia Encyclopedia.*

CHAPTER 6   Changes in Mrs. Booth, Asia, and John Wilkes: Ruggles, Smith. Edwin's continuing shyness: Smith. Anecdote about Mrs. Booth refusing to let Edwin have Junius's costumes: Kimmel. Edwin meets and falls in love with Mary Devlin: Ruggles, Kimmel, as excerpted from *Autobiography* by Joseph Jefferson (New York: The Century Company, 1889). Anecdote about Edwin wanting to be billed as "simply Edwin Booth": Ruggles. Impressions of Booth by Louisa May Alcott and Julia Ward Howe: Ruggles. Edwin's meeting and becoming friends with Adam Badeau: Smith, Ruggles. Edwin's up-and-down courtship of Mary Devlin and their engagement: Ruggles, Kimmel, Smith. Beginnings of John Wilkes Booth's stage career in Philadelphia and Richmond, and anecdote about his performance in *Lucretia Borgia*: Samples. Quote about John by actress Clara Morris: Samples, as excerpted from *Life on the Stage: My Personal Experiences and Recollections* by Clara Morris (New York: McClure, Phillips, 1901). Edwin's and John's appearance in *Richard III*, and Edwin's comments on his brother's acting: Samples. Background of John Brown: *Columbia Encyclopedia.* John Wilkes's impulsive decision to join the Richmond militia: Smith, Samples.

CHAPTER 7   John Wilkes at John Brown's execution: Smith, Kimmel, Ruggles, Samples. Marriage of Edwin and Mary Devlin: Ruggles. Election of 1860: *Columbia Encyclopedia.* John Wilkes's undelivered speech in support of the South: Rhodehamel and Taper. Abraham Lincoln and John Wilkes in Albany, N.Y.: Kimmel. Firing on Fort Sumter and the start of the Civil War: *Columbia Encyclopedia.* Mood of New York City in the opening months of the war: Ruggles. Knifing of John Wilkes by Henrietta Irving: Samples, Kimmel. Battle of Bull Run: *Columbia Encyclopedia.* Edwin's and Mary's departure for England: Ruggles.

CHAPTER 8 Edwin's experiences in England and the birth of his daughter Edwina: Ruggles, Kimmel. Battle of Antietam and Lincoln's decision to issue the Emancipation Proclamation: *Columbia Encyclopedia*. John's free-wheeling approach to acting, as recollected by Kate Reignolds: Samples, as excerpted from *Yesterdays with Actors* by Kate Reignolds (writing as Mrs. Catherine Mary Reignolds-Winslow) (Boston: Cupples & Ward, 1887). Boston critic's comment on John's misuse of his voice: Kimmel. Return of Edwin's drinking problem and Mary's concerns about it: Ruggles. Edwin's evaluation of John's acting: Smith, Ruggles. Boston critic's comparison of Edwin and John as performers: Smith. Edwin's drunken behavior in New York and Mary's worsening illness in Boston: Ruggles, as excerpted from Aldrich, Smith.

CHAPTER 9 Mary Devlin Booth's death and burial: Smith, Ruggles. Quote of Julia Ward Howe: Ruggles. Edwin's remorse and feelings of guilt: Smith, Ruggles, Kimmel. Mood of Washington in 1863: Smith. Anecdote about John's looking "sharp" at Lincoln: Smith, as excerpted from *The True Story of Mary, Wife of Lincoln* by Katherine Helm (New York: Harper & Brothers, 1928). John's anger with his brother-in-law, John Sleeper Clarke: Smith. Battle of Gettysburg: Catton, *Columbia Encyclopedia, The Long Road to Gettysburg* by Jim Murphy (New York: Clarion Books, 1992). Draft Riots in New York: Smith, *Columbia Encyclopedia*. Anecdote about John rescuing Adam Badeau: Smith. Scene between John and Asia in which he discloses his underground work for the South: Clarke.

CHAPTER 10 Edwin's return to the stage after Mary's death: Kimmel. John's higher fees and incessant touring in the fall of 1863: Samples, Rhodehamel and Taper. How John coped with travel delays due to Midwestern blizzard: Samples, Rhodehamel and Taper. The good-night poem Edwin recited to his daughter, Edwina: Ruggles. President Lincoln's reaction to Edwin's performance in *The Merchant of Venice*: Ruggles. Boston critic's enthusiastic response to John's acting in the spring of 1864: Samples. Stalemate in the Civil War in 1864 and doubts about President Lincoln: Catton, *Columbia Encyclopedia*. John's romantic involvement with Isabel Sumner: Rhodehamel and Taper. Union-Confederate prisoner-of-war exchange and John's plan to kidnap President Lincoln: Kimmel,

Smith, Ruggles, Hanchett. John's hatred of Lincoln, revealed in a conversation with Asia: Clarke. Edwin's plans to act with his two brothers in a benefit performance of *Julius Caesar*: Ruggles, Smith.

Chapter 11   Booth brothers star in *Julius Caesar*: Ruggles, Kimmel, Smith, Samples. The brothers' clash over Lincoln's reelection: Ruggles, Kimmel, Smith. Edwin's long-running production of *Hamlet*: Ruggles, Smith. John's fall 1864 letters, "To Whom It May Concern" and "To Mary Ann Holmes Booth": Rhodehamel and Taper. John's performance in Washington as Romeo, and his serious involvement with Lucy Hale: Smith. John's visit to Asia, during which he leaves a packet of papers with her: Clarke. Lincoln's second inauguration and John's reaction to the president's speech: Ruggles, Smith, Hanchett, Rhodehamel and Taper. Quote of Ann Hartley Gilbert about John's relationship with his mother: Samples, as excerpted from *The Stage Reminiscences of Mrs. Gilbert* by Ann Hartley Gilbert (New York: Scribner's, 1901). Mary Ann Booth's letter to John: Smith.

Chapter 12   Rejection of John's new kidnapping plan and failure of an alternate plan: Rhodehamel and Taper, Hanchett. John's final appearance as an actor: Samples. Civil War nears its end: Catton. John resorts to drink: Ruggles. Edwin's joyous words at war's end: Smith. John's furious reaction to Lincoln's support of voting rights for blacks: Smith, Ruggles, Hanchett. Booth hears that Lincoln and General Grant will be at Ford's Theatre the night of April 14: Ruggles, Smith, Kimmel, Steers, Reck. John's last dinner with Lucy Hale: Smith. Booth's plan to wipe out top government leaders with the aid of Lewis Powell and George Atzerodt: Rhodehamel and Taper, Hanchett. Events inside and outside Ford's Theatre leading up to assassination: Ruggles, Smith, Kimmel, Rhodehamel and Taper, Hanchett, Reck, Winik.

Chapter 13   John's and Davey Herold's escapes to Maryland: Steers. Atzerodt gets drunk, Powell goes on a rampage: Reck. Caring for the mortally wounded Lincoln: Reck. Asia's first reaction when she heard of the assassination: Smith, Ruggles, Clarke. June's response: Smith, Ruggles, Kimmel. Mary Ann Booth's hope that John will kill himself rather than be caught: Smith, Ruggles, as excerpted from Aldrich. Media attacks on the theater: Smith. Edwin's "stonelike" mood following the assassination: Smith, as excerpted from Aldrich.

CHAPTER 14 Revelation of Lucy Hale's relationship with John: Smith. Capture of John's fellow conspirators: Swanson and Weinberg. Booth and Herold's journey to Dr. Mudd's house and on to Colonel Cox's: Steers. President Lincoln's funeral: Winik. War Department poster offering rewards for Booth, Herold, and Surratt: Ruggles. John's diary entry, written while waiting to cross the Potomac: Rhodehamel and Taper. Departure of Lincoln's casket from Washington on its way back to Illinois: Winik. John and Davey's path through northern Virginia: Steers. John's thank-you note to Dr. Stewart: Rhodehamel and Taper. John and Davey's journey south to the Rappahannock River: Steers. Edwin's isolation in New York: Ruggles. John's arrival at the Garrett farm: Steers.

CHAPTER 15 Pursuit of John and Davey by a Union cavalry troop and their eventual discovery on the Garrett farm: Steers. John Wilkes Booth's death: Steers, Ruggles. How Mrs. Booth heard of her son's death: Smith, Ruggles, as excerpted from Aldrich. Asia's reaction to the news: Clarke, Ruggles. Quote from Edwin's letter to Asia about John: Smith. Letter from outraged citizen advising Edwin to leave the country: Smith. Ad taken by Edwin to express family's feelings: Smith. Quote from *New York Tribune* article urging that Edwin be judged on his own merits: Kimmel. Suggestion in *Philadelphia Press* that Edwin change his name: Smith.

CHAPTER 16 Transportation of John's body to Washington and confinement of his co-conspirators: Smith, Swanson and Weinberg. Lucy Hale's viewing of John's body: Smith. Preparations for the trial of the conspirators, newspaper reactions to the plans, conditions under which the conspirators were held, and the opening of the trial: Swanson and Weinberg. Edwin subpoenaed as a potential witness: Smith, Ruggles, Swanson and Weinberg. John Sleeper Clarke's prison experiences and the interrogation of Joseph Booth: Clarke. Quote from Edwin's letter to Emma Cary about the restoration of his good name: Grossman. End of the conspirators' trial, sentences meted out, and carrying out of the sentences: Swanson and

Weinberg. Quote from Edwin's letter to Emma Cary about his decision to resume his career: Kimmel, as excerpted from Grossman. Edwin's first attempt to reclaim John's body: Smith. Opposition of the *New York Herald* to Edwin's return to the stage: Ruggles.

Chapter 17   Edwin's return to the stage as Hamlet: Ruggles, Kimmel, Smith. His decision never to act again in Washington: Ruggles. Burning of the Winter Garden and Edwin's decision to build his own theater: Ruggles, Smith. Beginning of Edwin's involvement with Mary McVicker: Ruggles, Smith. Fresh attempts by Edwin to obtain John's remains: Smith, Ruggles. Departure of Asia and her family to England: Clarke, Ruggles. Problems with financing and construction of Booth Theatre: Ruggles. Opening of the Booth, praise for theater itself but criticism of Edwin's and Mary McVicker's performances in *Romeo and Juliet*: Smith, Ruggles. Edwin's final, successful attempt to secure John's body, and its burial in an unmarked grave in family's Baltimore plot: Smith, Ruggles. Marriage of Edwin and Mary McVicker: Ruggles.

Chapter 18   Birth and death of the Booths' son and Mary Booth's shaky mental state afterward: Ruggles. Mounting financial crisis of Booth Theatre: Ruggles, Smith. Burning of the contents of John's trunk: Smith, Ruggles, as excerpted from *Footlights and Spotlights: Recollections of My Life on the Stage* by Otis Skinner (New York: Bobbs-Merrill Company, Inc., 1924, 1972). Edwin forced to declare bankruptcy, and comments on his plight by friends and associates: Ruggles. Edwin's letters and poems to his daughter: Grossman. Contradictions in Mary McVicker Booth's personality: Ruggles. Edwin's annoyance with newspapers that describe him as "the brother of the man who killed Lincoln" and women who claim to have had serious relationships with John: Smith. Edwin's emergence from bankruptcy: Ruggles. Mary Booth's worsening condition: Ruggles.

Chapter 19   Attempt on Edwin's life: Ruggles, Smith. Edwin's trip to Europe and England with Mary and Edwina: Ruggles. Edwin invited to act with Henry Irving: Ruggles. Mary diagnosed with tuberculosis of the throat: Ruggles. Acclaim for Edwin and Irving's exchange of leading roles in *Othello*: Ruggles. Arrival of Mary's parents in London and departure of the McVickers and the Booths for America after conclusion of Edwin's engagement with Irving: Ruggles. Edwin's letter about John to historian Nahum Capen: Grossman. Edwin's enforced separation from Mary and her subsequent death: Ruggles.

CHAPTER 20   Edwin's private railroad car: Ruggles. Edwina's engagement to Downing Vaux and her second trip to England with her father: Ruggles, Watermeier. Praise for Edwin from a Dublin critic: Watermeier. Edwin's tour of Germany and Austria: Ruggles, Watermeier. Edwina's letter to William Winter about her father's performances: Watermeier. Decline in Downing Vaux's mental health and Edwina's resulting depression: Ruggles, Watermeier. End of Edwina's engagement to Vaux and her involvement with and marriage to Ignatius Grossman: Ruggles, Watermeier. Deaths of Edwin's brother June and then their mother: Ruggles, Smith. Edwin's collapse from vertigo during a performance of *Othello*: Ruggles. Edwina gives birth to a daughter, Mildred: Ruggles, Watermeier. Proposal by Lawrence Barrett that he and Edwin tour together: Ruggles, Watermeier.

CHAPTER 21   Kitty Malony's experiences on tour with Booth: Smith, Ruggles, as excerpted from *Behind the Scenes with Edwin Booth* by Katherine Goodale (Kitty Malony) (Boston: Houghton Mifflin Company, 1931). Idea for the Players: Ruggles, Smith, Kimmel. Incident in a Maine drugstore when druggist mentions John's name: Smith. Grand opening of the Players: Ruggles, Smith, Kimmel. Edwin's subsidies for deserving young club members: Smith. An attack of "nervous prostration" silences Edwin during a performance of *Othello*: Ruggles, Kimmel. Recordings Edwin made of Shakespearean speeches: Ruggles, and the author's impressions on hearing the recordings at New York Public Library. Negative reviews in New York for the aging Booth: Ruggles.

CHAPTER 22   Death of Lawrence Barrett: Ruggles, Kimmel. Edwin's farewell appearance as an actor: Ruggles, Kimmel. His final illness: Ruggles. Booth's last words: Grossman. His death, funeral, and burial: Ruggles.

INDEX

*Note: In this index, "J.W.B." refers to John Wilkes Booth. Page numbers in **bold** type refer to illustrations.*

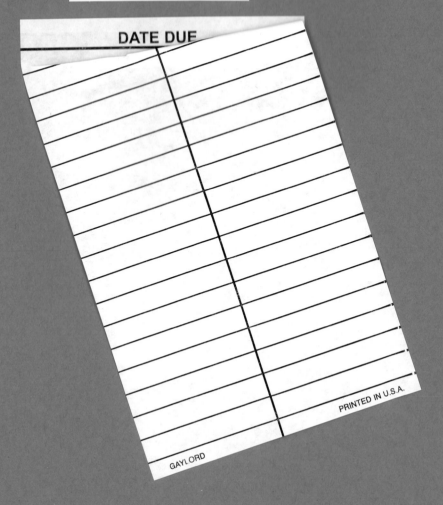

DATE DUE

PRINTED IN U.S.A.

GAYLORD